10 LIFE CHOICES

Recovering the Life
You Were Always
Meant to Live!

BOB PERDUE

🏠 CrossHouse

CrossHouse Publishing
P. O. Box 461592
Garland, TX 75046-1592
www.crosshousepublishing.org

ISBN: 978-1-934749-92-0
Library of Congress: 2010934559

To my wife Terri who has stood by me for over 30 years and been a living example of God's unconditional love and forgiveness.

This 2nd edition is dedicated to the memory of Michael Hunter

Acknowledgements
"Honor to whom honor is due"

Since *Ten Life Choices* has been a 5-year project, there have been so many whose lives and stories have impacted the message. I want to do my best to give honor to those people.

First, I thank my wife Terri who walked with me through this journey, modeled unconditional love and gave me loving feedback. She is the epitome of a precious daughter of the Father!

My parents gave me a solid foundation in a "God-consciousness" from which life has finally grown!

Doris Jackling, my #1 fan and encourager, who after 50 years of faithful ministry is now smiling down from heaven because I finally finished the book!

My original "band of brothers," Don, Rob, Jason, Steve, Kevin and Matt who "birthed" the Life Chart during a weekend retreat that none of us will ever forget.

My support team including friends, professional counselors and leaders of the Living Waters Program of Regeneration of Northern Virginia gave me the grace, love and community I needed to choose life after my suicide attempt. Thank you Bob, Al, Thomas, Jay, Don and John.

A big thank-you to the "sounding board" that helped to tweak *Ten Life Choices* including the Pastors I serve with: Steve, John, Aaron and Paul!

Those who helped in the editing, design and funding for the book also deserve a big thanks. These include Esther, Duane, Kris, Kathie and Tom.

My life has been enriched by all of these wonderful people. And now, they will enrich your life by their contribution to this book!

Table of Contents

CHAPTER 1

The Desire for Life

⌒✐⌒

Imagine yourself swimming in the ocean off of a beautiful beach. The sun is high overhead, the water is cool and refreshing, the seagulls are lazily swooping down for an occasional snack, and your two young children are playing at the edge of the surf, splashing and giggling. This is life! Suddenly, your peaceful revelry is shattered by one word from the lifeguard on the beach—SHARK! This single syllable conjures up images of blood, shredded flesh, and death (you've seen *Jaws*). Your reaction is immediate; get out of the water and get your children out of the water! Any parent that would continue swimming and allow their children to keep playing in the water would be assumed to be abnormal, negligent . . . even evil. The natural response in a situation which threatens immediate death is—choose life.

The man sitting in the cardiologist office is facing a decision. After a grueling series of tests and procedures, three blockages have been found in the arteries surrounding his heart. The doctor explains that a surgical procedure is necessary (code for "scalpel please"). They will remove a blood vessel from his leg and use it to bypass the blockages around his heart. As the doctor talks about the incision, the breaking of bones, etc., the man begins to realize that this is not going to be fun. His mind wanders and he begins to think, *I'd rather play golf.* In spite of his desire to avoid pain and deny the need for the surgery, his options become clear: have the surgery and live, or refuse the surgery and die. Presented with such clear options, the man opts for the surgery (You can't play golf if you are dead!). When it comes down to the wire, for all of his tough talk, he makes the obvious decision—choose life.

We are all born with a passion to live. Just think about the extraordinary measures that are taken to keep people alive who are suffering from terminal illness and the millions of dollars raised each year to help find a cure for cancer, heart disease, HIV and diabetes. We make rules and post signs about safety to try to minimize the number of people who die because of carelessness. *Wear your safety helmet. Don't drive over the speed limit. Don't drink and drive. Don't keep loaded guns near children.* These are all about life because we have a passion to live.

We are so passionate about life that we can't even force ourselves to talk about death. Euthanasia is not about killing people with terminal illness; it is a *quality of life* issue. Abortion is not about killing unborn babies; it is about *choice*, choosing the quality of the life of the mother and insisting that no life exists in the womb. The only one we cannot put a life spin on is suicide. So it is viewed as a mental health issue, one that is never discussed, even by those who have lived through the suicide of someone very close to them. Even at funerals, where death and mortality are staring us right in the face, we are uncomfortable with the discussion and want to move past the graveside service to the reception where we can eat potato salad and talk about shallow things. Life is clearly a more comfortable topic than death. We were not created for death; we were created for life.

> *We were not created for death; we were created for life.*

Every time I watch someone I love go through the valley of the shadow of death, I am more convinced that death is not what God intended for us. Several years ago, I sat by the bedside of a dear friend and mentor who was dying. She had given her life to God and served Him faithfully as a missionary in South America. I had the privilege of traveling back to Brazil with her, where the third generation of native Brazilians met to celebrate her life and ministry. Watching her struggle to breathe as the fluid filled her lungs, seeing the frailty of her arms and hands, being unable to communicate with her about how much she was loved, this was death. When she breathed her last, I went to my hotel room and reflected. Death is ugly, death is the opposite of life, and death is *not* what we were made for. We were made for life. God's first and most important instruction to man was choose life.

You are passionate about life! *Wait a minute, Bob, you don't even know me.* No, but I do know that you picked up this book—a book about choosing life.

There is something about the quality of your life that is not completely satisfying. There is something missing. I can almost hear the unspoken thoughts that are swirling around in your mind right now:

> *There has to be more to life than this.*
> *I need to get my life together.*
> *My life seems so empty and meaningless.*
> *I want to really live!*

The good news is that this desire—this innate passion for life—is God-given. You and I were created for life. When God, ". . . formed the man from the

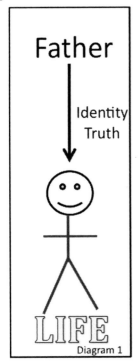

Diagram 1

dust of the ground and breathed into his nostrils the breath of life,"[1] man (Adam) came alive. He was connected to the life of God and then connected with the life of Eve when they became one flesh.[2] He was placed in a beautiful Garden surrounded by the living creation of God and given access to the tree of life. He was given beauty, provision, a dwelling place, excitement, adventure, responsibility, and pleasure and was free to enjoy it all. Here, surrounded by the newly created Garden and creatures, he was free to explore, discover, grow, enjoy, relate, reproduce, and achieve. What word would we use to describe all of that? *Life!* Not only did God breathe life into man, but then He set him up to live it to the fullest. No wonder we are passionate about life; our Creator is, too. We reflect God's passion for life because we were made in His image. This is the definition of life that is found in the writings of the Bible. Life is the connection between God and man that is experienced as a personal relationship between Creator and creature.

Connection with God is life. Through that connection, we know who we are, we reflect who He is, and we live in freedom out of our hearts. See Diagram 1 for an illustration of this life.

So, from the beginning, let's define what it is we are all really looking for. What is life? Life is a conscious, interactive, personal connection to our creator through which we get our true identity, experience peace and joy beyond circumstances, and sense a freedom to embrace our journey and connect with others from our hearts. This is the life we were created to enjoy. If this isn't what we are currently experiencing, the good news is that this life is available for us, and we have the power and the desire to choose it.

God didn't just create us for life; He also created us with a desire to *choose* life. After God breathed life into Adam and Eve and gave them the Garden of Eden and all that was in it to enjoy, he gave them another gift. He gave them the power to choose. There were two trees in that Garden that held special significance. One was the tree of life, and man was drawn to it. The other was the tree of the knowledge of good and evil. It represented man's independence from God. Taking of the fruit of that tree would make man the one who decides between good and evil, not God. In a sense, man would become *like God*. As we look back on this whole scenario, we ask ourselves why God would create the second tree. Why make death a possibility? Why even open the door to such a horrible outcome? Why give man a choice? The answer is that God created us, not just for life, but to *choose* life. God desires us to choose the life for which He created us. In that choice, He receives glory and honor above all else. It is important at the beginning of this journey that we take together that you understand this concept. Choosing life is what we were created to do. Choosing life brings honor and glory to God. Each life choice that is revealed in the later chapters of this book are opportunities for you to embrace the life you were always created to live and an opportunity for you to bring ultimate glory to God.

The free-will choice that God gave to Adam and Eve in the Garden was a clear choice between life and death. The tree of life was always accessible. The forbidden fruit from the tree of knowledge of good and evil which would lead to death was also a viable option. Every day in the Garden of Eden, the first man and woman were faced with the choice of life or death. God gave them the free will to choose, but He also gave them valuable information about the consequences of their choice. Their choice would not be made out of ignorance. He told them if they ate of that tree, they would die—simple, direct, and understandable, with no ifs, ands or buts . . . death! The desire for life was actually enhanced by the possibility of death and by God's warning. Their God-given desire for life kept them as far from that tree as they could get. Consider this, every day I take a certain medication for a health condition. The medication greatly enhances the quality of my life by making up for something my body is lacking. Every time I take this medicine, I am choosing life. This same medicine, if taken to excess, could result in death. There are warnings on the bottle about taking too much. The truth is that I have the power to choose whether to take the recommended dose or to take an overdose. Every day, I get to choose between life and death. Knowing that the right amount is life and making the choice to take the right amount each day, actually empowers me. It makes me conscious of choosing life in a way that I wouldn't if I didn't have to take the medication at all. Adam and Eve needed visible symbols of their desire to choose life. So, God who gave them life and gave them a second gift—the power to choose life—also gave them visible reminders of that choice. The two trees in the Garden reminded Adam and Eve every day that they had the power and the opportunity to choose life. We all have the same power, and we all have visible reminders of that choice. For us, it is not two trees. But it may be a bottle of Jack Daniels and a bottle of water; a cigarette and a piece of sugarless gum; an x-rated Internet site and a picture of our family; a large crème-filled donut and a carrot stick; or another hour of gossip on the phone and another hour of intimate conversation with our Creator. This power to choose life is clearly foundational to our humanity but misunderstood and under-utilized. Would it be redundant to say choose life?

The *fall of man* into sin is a really poor way to explain what actually happened in that Garden. Adam and Eve *chose* sin and death over life. Before we are too hard on them, think about your own choices. No one pushed them, they didn't trip over anything, they weren't forced; they just chose. Although no time table is provided for us in Scripture, it seems reasonable to assume that Adam and Eve enjoyed life with God in the Garden of Eden for some time before the events that led to their downfall in Genesis 3. They walked with God in the cool of the day for weeks, months, maybe even years. The daily decision to choose life was the natural flow until Satan entered the picture. Up to this point, man's God-given desire for life ruled his choice, and he chose the tree of life. Satan had been separated from God (death) because he chose his own way over God's. Now he wanted to lead God's creation down that same path. But Satan was crafty; he knew that Adam and Eve were created with a great desire for life and that he would never be able to talk them into eating of the tree of knowledge of good and evil by trying to sell them on death. So Satan's scheme to deceive Eve into sin was not to make death attractive to her, but to redefine life for her. He knew that God created them with a passion for life, and he was going to use that passion to tempt them away from God. Satan convinced Eve that partaking of the forbidden fruit would not end in her immediate death (". . . you will not surely die . . .")[3] but would actually lead to a better life (". . . you will be like God . . .").[4] He used her desire for life to rob her of life. Unfortunately, the better life that Satan promised never really panned out, and his empty promises continue today through ad agencies, politicians, and long-winded preachers! The truth is that there is no better life than the one that God offers. It's too bad we can't interview Adam at this point. Satan has been using the same scheme of redefining life and leading men away from life ever since. He tells us that life is in the party, in the good feeling, in the sex, in the money, and in the power. The result is always the same—death. The Bible put it this way: "There is a way that seems right to a man, but in the end it leads to death."[5] Material possessions, power, sexual fulfillment, and pleasure have been used by Satan for millennia to redefine life. Sadly, we continue to *fall* (the code word for choose) for his deceit and into his trap. In a later chapter we will spend some time on the phenomena of looking for life in all the wrong places.

After man chose to go it on his own, God's desire remained the same. Man chose death but God offers life—again. The redemptive plan God announced first to Adam and Eve was that the "seed of the woman" would rescue us from death and give us life.[6] God's first offer of grace, His first promise of redemption was all about life. But how? He had clearly stated that the consequence of their poor choice was death and this price must be paid. God instituted a system of sacrifice where an animal was killed to provide a covering for Adam and Eve's nakedness and shame (the first death). The penalty for man's choice (death) would be assumed by a spotless animal whose blood was shed as a symbolic substitute for the death of man. This sacrificial system was merely a shadow, looking forward to the ultimate price to be paid for man's sin: the death of God's own son, Jesus. The personal decision of each individual in that day to sacrifice the animal according to God's system was a decision to choose life. In the same way the personal decision of each individual today to receive by faith the complete sacrifice of Christ for his or her sin is a decision to choose life. God's gracious offer of a redemptive plan is focused on life.

So it began and so it continues. The early history of mankind after the choice to sin as recorded in Genesis, the first book of the Bible, is an account of people choosing life or choosing death. Cain, the first son of Adam and Eve, chose his own way and offered a bloodless sacrifice. It made sense to him. He was deciding what was good and evil now, which was to offer the fruits of his own labors (vegetables from his Garden) as a sacrifice to God. Cain chose to ignore God's requirement and approach Him in a way that seemed right to him. There was no real difference between his choice and the choice of Adam and Eve. He chose to do life his own way, not God's. In essence, Cain chose death rather than life. His choice led him down a path of death, which included the murder of his own brother Abel[7] and personal alienation from the world of life.[8] Several generations later, Noah made a choice for life when he chose to do life God's way. He risked his life and reputation by building an ark and save the whole human race from God's judgment for no better reason than because God said so. This was clearly a life choice. When the flood waters finally subsided and Noah emerged from the ark, he chose to offer the sacrifice that God requited—a blood sacrifice—as an act of re-establishing the relationship between God and man. The life was in the blood and the shedding of that blood was a choice for life. The price for man's sin choice was covered by the giving of the life of the animal. Before the flood, man had become alienated from God because of a sinful lifestyle (death). But after the flood, Noah reconnected man to God through the offering of the sacrifice that would cover the sin and reconnect us to God (life). Of course, the blood of a spotless animal was powerless to take away sin.[9] But the offering of the sacrifice became a symbol of man following God's original design, choosing the path of life, until He could send the perfect sacrifice that would take away sin forever.[10]

Choosing to accept Jesus' sacrifice is choosing life.

Jesus was sent as the perfect Lamb of God that ". . . takes away the sin of the world."[11] Choosing to accept Jesus' sacrifice is choosing life. This is the whole reason that Jesus was sent, so that we would have the opportunity once again to choose life at any moment. Jesus' message was a message of life. Consider His words:

". . . I have come that they may have life and have it to the full."[12]

". . . I am the resurrection and the life. He who believes in me will live, even though he dies."[13]

"Jesus answered, 'I am the way and the truth and the life. No one comes to the Father except through me.'"[14]

Because of Jesus' sacrifice for sin, we can choose life. Life becomes an every-moment possibility for us. The death which came as a result of man's poor choice in the Garden was completely experienced by Jesus on our behalf. He bore our sin and He bore our death. In return, He gives us life; life—not just Heaven—but eternal life, which begins now and includes a reconnection and personal relationship with our Creator, our Father. We are back in the Garden, walking with God in the cool of the day. We know who we are; we are a reflection of who He is. We know what our purpose is. We know we are never alone. We know how to live in authentic relationship with others. Life!

Salvation then becomes a perfect balance between God's gracious gift (the sacrifice of Christ) and our choice (faith in Christ's sacrifice). This balance is beautifully portrayed in a book of the Bible written by the Apostle Paul to the early believers in Ephesus. He writes, "For it is by grace that you have been saved, through your faith. It is not of your own doing, your own works, so that no one can boast."[15] If we choose Jesus, we choose life. Any attempts that are made to choose life apart from Jesus are the futile strivings of man and will either completely fail or leave us with a list of coping mechanisms that make our pseudo-life one of striving with no rest. True life is found in connection with the One who gave us life in the beginning, and only Jesus can reconnect us to Him. Jesus said, "I am the way and the truth and the life. No one comes to the Father except through me."[16] Because of Jesus, life is an every-moment possibility.

These biblical facts leave us with a question. If God created and designed us with an overwhelming desire for life, and He has provided us with the opportunity to choose life at any moment by choosing Christ, why do so many still feel like they are missing life? Why do so many people struggle from addiction to addiction? Why are we unable to live in authentic relationships that work? Why do we jump from church to church looking for answers? Why is there so much searching for something that should be so easy to find? As I said, you picked up this book because in some way, you are still searching for life. Picking up this book was a choice for life. The good news is that life is an option that we are free to choose. Choose life! Read on.

Chapter 1—Questions to Ponder

1. Think of a situation in your life when you engaged your will to choose life when death was a possibility. What thoughts were going through your mind at that time?

2. Have you ever said things like:
   "There has to be more to life than this;"
   "I need to get my life together;"
   "My life is so empty and meaningless;"
   "I want to really live"?

Put the message of your own heart into words and write it below:

This statement is a message that arises out of your God-given passion for life. Are you willing to begin to make that connection?

3. What ways has Satan tried to redefine life for you? How is that working for you so far?

4. What do you really believe about Jesus and why He came to earth?

5. If you have a desire to quit this process, which statement below best defines the reason:
   _____ I am really not that broken.
   _____ I don't want to talk about my past with anyone else.
   _____ I don't really believe that God can heal me.
   _____ I am afraid of the emotions I will have to face
   _____ Other: _____

6. From where do you think the thought above is coming?

CHAPTER 2

The Search for Life

◦♊◦

S everal years ago, some friends rented a beach house for my family in Ocean City. They picked the house and sent me an e-mail with a picture and street address. As the trip grew closer, my preparations included going on MapQuest, entering the address, and mapping out a route. My first attempt yielded a message which read "no such address found." Thinking that surely I had just mistyped some part of the address, I made a second attempt with the same results. I certainly couldn't give up my search after two attempts. After all, a beach vacation was at stake. A Google search led me to a street map of Ocean City. My plan was to find the street and then figure the best route from there. I scoured that map for quite some time looking for that street name, but it didn't appear to be there. Now, I was getting frantic. I started to call the Ocean City Chamber of Commerce when it suddenly occurred to me that I should go back to the original source of my information, the e-mail from my friend, to see what I might be missing. There at the source, I found the answer. The beach house was in Ocean City, NJ, and I had been searching Ocean City, MD. All of my diligence, passion, expertise, and persistence made no difference as long as I was searching in the wrong place.

This illustrates perfectly why we can't seem to find the life that will completely satisfy us. It also reminds us that the admonition to *choose life* will do no good if we have no idea where life is found. Remember that Satan's scheme to lead us from life is to offer us a better life that is actually death in disguise. So many things appeal to our flesh and look like life. Satan has an easy job of side-tracking us. Looking for life in all the wrong places has led us to many dead ends, disappointments, and heartbreaks. Life is at stake! Rather than give up our search, let's go back to the source of life to find out what life is really all about.

In the previous chapter, we observed that life can be traced back to God. He literally breathed life into Adam's lifeless form. Adam's first experiences of life were his experiences relating to God in the perfect environment in the Garden of Eden. But God wanted more for Adam. In fact, Adam needed something more, for it was declared that his present state was *not good.*[17] Adam needed to share this relationship that he had with God with another, like himself. The problem was that Adam was oblivious to his own need. Does that sound familiar? So God brought the animals before Adam to be named. Each animal came in a pair (male and female), but no suitable partner was found for Adam.[18] However, the experience did have the desired result; Adam was left with a new realization . . . I need. It was only after the realization of his need that Adam signed the consent form for the surgery that led to the creation of Eve.

The creation of Eve was God's provision for Adam so that he might enjoy and share this relationship with God in a new dimension, the dimension of community. God had eternally existed in the community of the trinity and had a shared relationship between Father, Son, and Holy Spirit. Now, His creation mirrored that same community. Man, in relationship with God, sharing that relationship with another was a reflection of God Himself. It was life. God was walking with them in the cool of the day,[19] affirming who they were, teaching them, loving them, and allowing them to love and worship Him. This was the choice that Adam was free to make every day, the choice to stay in relationship with God and share that relationship with Eve. This was choosing life.

Do you see it? When you choose to live daily in a personal, interactive relationship with God and with others, you are choosing life. Any attempt to find life in anything else is sin. In fact, this is the most basic definition of sin that we have, looking for life in something other than God.

George felt that he would feel good about himself and be able to really enjoy life if he climbed the corporate ladder, made a name for himself, and was able to buy whatever his heart desired. Sure, he had become disillusioned along the way, when this desire for life caused him to lose his family and left him no time for meaningful relationship. He was driven to find life—a God-given passion—but he was looking for it in the wrong place. Upon entering retirement, with his title and possessions exceeding even his own goals, he told me that his life was empty and meaningless, and he was struggling with a deep depression. Life cannot be found in things.

Marlene was distraught because her daughter had moved in with her boyfriend. She had raised her in church and taught her the difference between right and wrong. She had emphasized the importance of purity before marriage. Marlene was sure that her daughter was doing all of this just to hurt her. How could she go to church and hold up her head when others knew what her daughter was doing? God had failed her. How could she go on practicing her faith when she wasn't sure she could count on God at all? Marlene was trying to get life out of her daughter. In order for Marlene to be okay, to enjoy and embrace life, her daughter *must* make right choices. You cannot find life in other people.

Corey was adamant that he was not going to live *like the Amish.* He was tired of the strict standards of his parents and church. He was on his own now, and he was going to *live a little.* Partying with friends, casual sexual encounters, fast driving, and loose spending were going to bring him life. Even while he was insisting that this was really living, he was unwilling even to consider changing his ways. He admitted that there was always an empty feeling after the party in the down moments of his life. Knowing many who have walked this path, if he survives to be in his 30's, he will have to face the fact that this is not life.

Sandra was a different story. She was going to live her life for God. She volunteered at church and did such a good job that whenever a new ministry or project came up, the leadership called on Sandra and she always pulled through. She worked night and day to keep up with her church commitments, but spent very little time with God in a personal relationship. She greatly enjoyed the praise she received from people at church. When the church had a major community event and chose someone else to lead the congregation in preparation, she was devastated. What had she done wrong that they would choose someone else? Did they not appreciate all that she had done? She came into my office heartbroken. Sandra was trying to get life out of religious performance, and she was realizing that church is *not* the source of life.

This journey back to the source of life shows clearly that life, real life, satisfying life, is found in relationship with God. I can hear many who are reading this heave a heavy, disappointing sigh. *I've tried that, it didn't work. I have been in relationship with God for years and still feel dissatisfied, unfulfilled.* Let me challenge you. Have you really tried an intimate relationship with God, or was it a relationship with religion or church? Did you enter into a system of belief, or did you enter into an actual relationship with the Heavenly Father who is the source and essence of life and who longs to walk with you in the cool of the day?

Unfortunately, it is probably true that Christianity has spoiled the Christian's view of life. I believe that Christianity is, in its most basic form, an invitation to choose life by entering into an intimate relationship with God the Father through the gracious sacrifice of Christ *and* the opportunity to choose to walk in that life every moment of every day.

In support of this claim, let us look at two definitive statements made by Christ. First, consider these words of Jesus, "Come to me, all you who are weary and burdened, and I will give you rest."[20] This is an invitation. We are invited *into* something, not compelled to obey something, or asked to recite something, or forced to adhere to something, but invited. Christianity is an invitation.

This is an invitation to join Christ in a relationship. Jesus says, "Come to me . . .." This is not an invitation to an institution or a system of belief but an invitation to a person, an invitation to a relationship.

The invitation is being extended to a particular group of people, the weary and burdened. Those who have needs and *know* they have needs are invited. Just like Adam, many are oblivious to their needs and thus see no reason to enter into a relationship with God. Realization of need is the first step toward God. This realization is called confession or repentance. Jesus said if we don't repent, we will all perish (death, not life).[21] He also said that if we consider ourselves well (with no needs), we will not seek the help of the physician.[22] Are you weary and burdened? What is it that is weighing you down? What is it that you really need? Life. Looking for life in all of the wrong places is exhausting

> *Christianity is, in its most basic form, an invitation to choose life by entering into an intimate relationship with God the Father through the gracious sacrifice of Christ and the opportunity to choose to walk in that life every moment of every day.*

you, and trying to protect yourself *from* life after being hurt is equally exhausting. The day that Jesus verbally offered this invitation, He was looking out on a society of people that was striving hard to find life through a system of law and works. God had given His people a list of commands (10 in all) which the religious leaders had expanded to several hundred. The Pharisees were not looking for life in people, they were looking for the flaws. The question was *how have you broken the law today?* This constant scrutiny of every aspect of life was exhausting. Jesus saw their plight and He offered them rest. He offers the same to us. He doesn't want us to approach His Word or His Church with the question, *what is wrong with me?* or *how am I offending God today?* He wants us to approach His Word and His Church in order to maintain and improve our personal relationship with Him, to draw nearer. The invitation of Christianity is an invitation into a relationship with Jesus that will stop all of our striving for life because we will find that life in Him. If Jesus is life and He comes into our lives when we invite Him, we no longer need to prove our identity. Jesus is our identity. We no longer need to strive to be acceptable to God. Jesus makes us acceptable to God. We no longer need to strive to do righteous deeds; Jesus has made us righteous. Jesus is our life.

Unfortunately, in today's church, it is easy to hear the invitation and enter into a system of belief instead of a relationship. Followers of Christ who are still trying to please God through wearing the right clothes, carrying the right Bible, and shunning the *worldly* behaviors, are not experiencing the rest that Jesus offered because they are not experiencing the life that comes from a relationship. Finding Jesus is finding life, and finding life automatically ends our striving for life. We enter into . . . rest.

But I still struggle with sin. (I knew you wanted to interrupt me at this point.) Scripture is clear that our old sinful nature died with Christ on that cross[23] and though that part of us is dead, we are still alive because Christ lives through us.[24] In Christ we have a new heart, a good heart that desires life through Christ.[25] Any struggle that we have with sin is not coming from our true self; it is coming from sin that lives in us. It is coming from our flesh, which has been trained by the world around us and our own selfish desires before Christ. Even the Apostle Paul had these flesh struggles. But he did not define himself by the struggle. Instead he attributed the struggle to sin in him and claimed the ultimate victory through Christ who was His life.[26] So, when Christ invites us into relationship with Him, He invites us to let Him be our life so that we can stop striving to find life in all of the wrong places . . . rest.

Now let us move on from this invitation to another statement made by Christ. Jesus also said, "I am the way and the truth and the life. No one comes to the Father except through me."[27] Jesus is the way, not the destination. He offers us the way to life. Where is this way taking us? It is taking us to the Father. No one comes to the Father, except through Jesus. Jesus' death on the cross was not accomplished just to get us to the cross to repent of our sin and gain forgiveness. It was not our *get-out-of-Hell-free* card. It was not to convert us from heathen to Christian. It was not to make us a member of the church. It was accomplished to take us by way of the cross to the Father, because in the presence of the Father we find life. Now, once we find life in Him, we are exempted from eternity in Hell. We become Christ-followers and are a part of His body, *the Church*. But that is not the point. The point is that we are reconnected to the Father.

Many followers of Christ spend their whole Christian experience wallowing at the cross, striving against sin, trying to overcome guilt, shame, and condemnation—examining life by the law and always coming up short or trying to earn points with God by being pious. Jesus did not die so that we could continue to strive against sin. He died so that we could be freed from sin, declared righteous, and be ushered into the presence of the Father. We can enter boldly into the presence of the Father and find help for all of our needs.[28] Entering into the presence of the Father takes us back to what God created us for . . . life. This is exactly what is promised for those who believe in Jesus.

". . . whoever believes in Him will not perish but have eternal life."[29]

"He who has the Son has life . . ."[30]

". . . whoever lives and believes in me will never die."[31]

Everlasting life is not Heaven. Everlasting life is a reconnection with the Father into a relationship where He walks with us in the cool of the day like He did with Adam. We are conscious of our connection to Him, our greater purpose, our power to choose, and our capacity to love from our hearts deeply. He gives us a new identity, not according to our sin, and He affirms that identity in us. He fully accepts and forgives us and holds no condemnation over our heads. We are free from sin, the law, and our own past. There is no more striving in His presence. There is no more fear of death in His presence. There is no shame in His presence. This is life. This life will last forever, so it will include the time we live in Heaven. It also includes the time from the moment we accept His invitation until the moment we breathe our last on this earth. Through Jesus (the Way), we can have life now.

Jacob was referred to me by his family because his wife had caught him looking at pornography on the Internet. He sat in the chair across from me with his head down. He was a believer in Christ but he was not experiencing life. As he shared with me in that first session, it became apparent that Jacob took his identity from his sin. He was a loser and a pervert because of the things that he looked at on his computer. He also believed that he was powerless to stop the behavior. He kept asking what was wrong with him. When I began to talk with Jacob about his relationship with God, he got annoyed with me. He said "What does this have to do with my addiction?" I was so glad that he asked. I gently explained to Jacob that, as a believer, he was a righteous man, a child of the Father, and accepted by God in spite of his behaviors. His identity was completely found in Christ, who was alive in Him. Because this was true, he had the power to choose to live out of that identity and completely surrender the need to look at pornography. He asked if he should get accountability for his Internet problems, but I counseled him to get accountability for his time with the Father. That is where he would find life, and that is where he would find the power over his addiction.

Can you see that Jesus made it clear the opportunity to choose life is an every-moment possibility? It all seems so simple when we see Christ as our life. But if life has been provided for us through Christ, what keeps us from choosing and experiencing this life consistently? If we have a built-in desire for life and if God has provided the way to life, why are so many still striving for it?

A clue to the answer is found in the experience of Adam and Eve. They were experiencing life by relationship with the Father when they were tempted by the serpent to partake of the tree of knowledge of good and evil. They did not have a death wish. They did not consciously feel that they were choosing death when they gave in to the temptation and tasted the forbidden fruit. Satan had crafted the temptation in such a way that they actually felt they were pursuing life by eating the fruit. Satan told them if they ate of it, they would be like

God. The only thing that might be better than life would be more life. Being like God was an appeal to their desire for more life. The problem was they were now looking for life in a place other than God. As we said earlier, this is the essence of sin. They were taking a detour from God's plan for life and striking out on their own for a better experience. As time has passed from that original detour, many other detours have been taken. Any time we look for life in a place other than God, we are on a detour. Let's examine the detours most commonly taken to find life and see where we may have gone astray. Choose life! Read on.

Any time we look for life in a place other than God, we are on a detour.

Chapter 2—Questions to Ponder

1. Have you come to the place where you realize your deepest need? If so, put that need into words in the form of a prayer to the Father and write it out below.

2. Has your experience with Christianity been more like an invitation into a relationship or an invitation into a system of belief? Explain.

3. What evidence of *striving for life* is still present in your experience? From what things, people, or circumstances are you trying to get life?

4. Have you had an experience with God at the cross of Jesus? Write about that experience below.

5. Can you now hear the voice of the Father inviting you into relationship . . . into rest?

CHAPTER 3

Detours from Life

～

Years ago I took a group of teenagers to New York City on a mission trip. I drove an old 15-passenger van and pulled a trailer full of sleeping bags and luggage through Brooklyn. What a scene! After our initial meeting at the church, I got detailed directions on how to navigate my classy vehicle from the church to the pastor's home where I would be staying. There were quite a few turns involved, but I am proud to say that due to my giftedness in navigation, I made it without a problem. The next year, I returned to the same church with my teens. This time when I left the church for the pastor's home, I informed him I did not need directions. I remembered the turns from the previous year and would meet the pastor and his family back at their house. When I finally parallel-parked my van on the pastor's street, he was sure that I had been lost in the city since it had taken me so much longer to get there. He inquired about my route, and I described the way I had come. He began laughing and explained that a major road had been closed the year before so he had to direct me to his house via a detour. The actual directions involved only one turn. I had no idea that I was driving through a detour, because I was clueless about the true way to his house.

I believe that many of us, though Christians, are not satisfied with life. We are confused because we believe we are on the right way to life and don't even realize that we are on a detour. We have put our faith in Christ. We go to church. We read our Bible. We even serve God in the church. But this is not life. Do you remember how we defined life in the previous chapters? Life is an intimate relationship with God. God created us in His image and He made us His sons and daughters. He gave us a good heart, and He longs to commune

31

with us as He did with Adam and Eve. This interactive, affirming, ongoing relationship with the Father is called life (refer to Diagram 1 in Chapter 1). Because our heart is good and we are unconditionally loved, we are free in this place to live out of and trust our hearts. We are free to express ourselves, to grow, to explore, to risk, to question, and free to live. Life becomes an expression of what is in our hearts. This is the true self, the self as God intended it. This is the life we were always meant to live. This is the self we were always meant to be. This is the life we desire and the life God urges us to choose.

One of the wonderful benefits of living in relationship with the Father is that He gives us a positive identity.

One of the wonderful benefits of living in relationship with the Father is that He gives us a positive identity. We know who we are and it is good. This positive identity differs from what psychologists call positive self-esteem. Self-esteem is about how I feel about myself; positive identity is about who I really am. In the book, *We Weep for Ourselves and for our Children*, the authors define positive identity with four major components[32] (see Diagram 2):

1) **Virtue.** This is the sense that we have spiritual value and worth. Our value is inherent in the fact that we are created in the image of God. It is not derived from the good things we do for God. God created Adam and Eve and then called them good. What had they done to deserve that affirmation? Nothing. Their goodness was a part of the way God made them, their true self. Knowing our true value is a vital part of a positive identity.

2) **Community.** This is the sense that we belong and are a part of something bigger than ourselves, that we have something to offer. God created us ("let us make man . . .")[33] *out of* community and He created us *for* community ("it is not good for man to be alone . . .")[34]. An infant is *we* with its mother before he or she becomes an *I*. Knowing that you belong to a caring community is a vital part of a positive identity.

3) **Power.** This is the sense that we have choices and the ability to choose. We have already established that God created us with a choice and with the power to make that choice. Limits to our power by God-given boundaries help

keep our power from destroying our virtue. Knowing that we have the power to make good choices is a vital part of a positive identity.

4) **Gender.** This is the sense that we are masculine or feminine and comfortable with our sexuality. God specifically created mankind as "male and female."[35] The difference between the genders is a part of the design. The unique ways that God created men and women allow them to complement each other as they move together toward intimacy. Knowing our gender and being comfortable with our masculinity or femininity is a vital part of a positive identity.

Positive Identity

Virtue (spiritual value) I am good/valuable	Community I am loved/I am a part of
Power I have choices/I have what it takes	Sexuality/ Gender I am male/female

Diagram 2

Since all four of these qualities are part of the true self that God created us to be, it stands to reason that any movement away from these qualities is a good indication we have taken a detour from life. In fact, any time we move away from life, our positive identity suffers because we are trying to find life in something other than God. Since God gives us our positive identity, we lose sight of it as we wander from Him. Therefore, these components of positive identity become a good criterion for judging whether we are living in this intimate relationship with God called life.

This is a good time for us to pause and ask a few probing questions. Do I understand my true value as a person or do I tend to base my value on performance or behavior? Do I enter fully into community and feel a part of something bigger than myself, or do I tend to isolate from others and perform at public functions? Do I carefully use my power to make good choices, or do I wield my power carelessly? Do I tend to play the powerless victim, or do I try to use my power to control all of those around me? Am I comfortable with my masculinity or femininity, or do I tend to act as though I have something to prove in that area? Life and positive identity go hand in hand. This is the way we can regularly take inventory of our lives.

Our tendency, though, is to judge the quality of our life by other criteria. Am I happy? Am I getting what I want? Am I achieving all of my goals? These criteria actually grow out of a view of God as a resource to make my life work the way I think it should rather than viewing God as life itself.

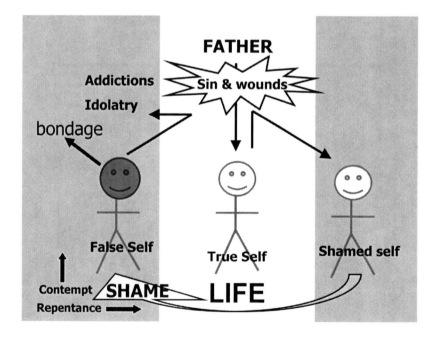

Diagram 3 is going to serve as our Life Chart for the rest of this study. It resembles a map which we can use to chart where we are in our relationship with God and pinpoint some of the detours we have taken. In the Garden of Eden, Adam and Eve lived out of their true selves and enjoyed this kind of relationship with God. He was their life and they enjoyed life . . . until sin (see the center of the Life Chart). Sin separates us from God and interrupts the relationship called life[36] (see Sin on the Life Chart in Diagram 3). Since we were all born into sin, we were born outside of the experience of life that God intends for us. As sinners, without life but still created in the image of God with the God-given passion for life, we are driven to try to find life. Our individual sins grow out of the many ways we try to find or get life out of things other than God. Unfortunately, this attempt to find life just increases the separation. Our original sin, inherited from Adam, separated us from life and our own sin furthers the separation. The separation caused by these sins makes it impossible for us to see ourselves as a reflection of the Father, created in His image. Instead, we begin to see ourselves as a reflection of our sin (see Perception of Shamed Self in Diagram 3).

Complicating this scenario is the introduction of wounds (see Wounds on the Life Chart in Diagram 3). Wounds are sins that are committed against us by others. Wounds include all forms of abuse, rejection, abandonment, and neglect. They carry with them specific attacks on our positive identity.

1) As wounded persons, we do not feel valued; the violation of our personhood by another leaves us feeling abused and worthless. Our sense of value is damaged and we begin to strive to prove that we are okay (performance), or we sink into the realization that we have no value (victim).

2) Since wounds are usually inflicted by someone who is in our community, such as a trusted family member, authority figure or friend, the sense of community is shattered by an overwhelming feeling of distrust. We cannot be a part of the community because we cannot trust anyone to get too close. Our sense of community is damaged, and we begin either to isolate from people or develop a public persona that people will accept. There is more on this later in the chapter.

3) In our wounding, we usually experience being overpowered by the one who inflicted the wound. Things happened, such as abuse, abandonment, rejection, or humiliation, which were outside of the realm of our control. We felt we had no power. The result is that the sense of power is adversely affected. We either react by giving up all power and letting others rule us completely as victims, or we develop the attitude that we must always be in control in order to be okay.

4) Sexual wounding, through abuse, exposure to inappropriate sexual situations or images, or an imbalance in parental involvement between masculine and feminine, causes confusion about sexuality. Gender confusion, same-sex attractions, rejection of sex, or obsession with sex are all results of a loss of sexual identity through wounding. Men who are wounded this way may overcompensate and become overly masculine to prove their gender or become passive men. They also may reject their gender altogether and move toward homosexuality. Women who are wounded in this way may overcompensate by becoming overly feminine and syrupy sweet, militant about proving women's equality with men, or may reject their femininity and move toward homosexuality.

Let's pause here for a moment and look at the Life Chart. Do you tend to see yourself as the person in the middle of the chart, living out of your heart with a positive identity? Do you tend to see yourself as the person on the right-hand side of the chart, living as a reaction to your sin and wounds with a broken identity? If you see yourself on the right-hand side of the chart, which parts of the positive identity have been broken for you? Identifying these things at the beginning of this process will aid you greatly as you move forward to choose life.

Our sin and wounds separate us from the affirming voice of God and thus from our positive identity. We are left in confusion about who we really are. In this void, the powerful voice of our sin and wounds rises up to put a label on us—a label that identifies us or connects us with our sin and wounds. The self-talk that is going on in our minds tells us:

I am a pervert.
I am a failure.

I am gay.
I am inadequate.
I am so undisciplined.
I am a terrible parent.
I am a disappointment.
I am a loser.
I am damaged goods.
I am stupid.

These labels and many more represent the false perception of self that we may adopt because of our sin and wounds. The labels that we wear are reinforced by the lies of the Enemy that circulate in our minds as more negative self-talk:

I'll never amount to anything.
I will never overcome this habit.
I don't really have anything to offer others.
If people knew who I really was, they wouldn't want to be with me.

Satan is the father of all lies[37] and both introduces and fuels these lies. In time, these lies build up a stronghold in our minds and empower the label we have chosen. We not only become what we fear we are, we also act out of that identity.

I received a phone call one day from Sheryl, a beautiful young mother of three. She barely made it through one sentence without breaking down and sobbing into the telephone. The only statement that I could understand amidst the sobs was, *I am a terrible mother.* When Sheryl came in, she began to share how she couldn't seem to love her children the way other mothers did. She didn't want to hold them or hug them. They wanted to cling to her and she wouldn't allow it. She saw other mothers cuddling their children and knew that this was what she *should* do; she must be a bad mother. As we talked about her relationship with the Father, she finally shared that years before as a teenager, she had an abortion. It was obvious from her sharing that she was completely broken over this poor choice made in a desperate situation. What she did not realize is that she had accepted a label out of that sin. What kind of mother would kill her unborn baby? A terrible mother would. She had labeled herself a terrible mother before she ever gave birth to her first child. Her identity was coming from her sin, and now she was living out of that identity. Sheryl had to make several life choices in order to cast off this label and begin to believe in who she really is, a precious daughter of the Father and a loving mother.

The separation from the affirming voice of God and the powerful message of the labels and lies quickly convince us of our negative identity. The end result of embracing this negative identity is a deep sense of shame (see Shame on the Life Chart). Shame is defined as the overwhelming feeling that there is *something wrong with me. Other people are okay and have it together but not me.* Lewis Smedes, in his book, *Shame and Grace,* has this to say about shame:

> "The feeling of shame is about our very selves—not about some thing we did or said but about what we are. It tells us that we are unworthy. Totally. It is not as if a few seams in the garment of our selves need stitching; the whole fabric is frayed. We feel that we are unacceptable. And to feel that is a life-wearying heaviness. Shame-burdened people are the sort whom Jesus had in mind when he invited the 'weary and heavy laden' to trade their heaviness for his lightness."[38]

Shame is defined as the overwhelming feeling that there is something wrong with me.

Shame is an extremely powerful emotion that works its way out in our lives in various ways. The first possible response to shame is repentance. Adam and Eve experienced shame when they sinned against God in the Garden.[39] God's subsequent conversation with them seems to indicate that the purpose of their shame was to lead them to repentance. He asked them questions He already knew the answers to in order to get them to admit their mistake and seek forgiveness. *Where are you? Who told you that you were naked? Did you eat the forbidden fruit?*[40] God knew the answers to these questions; He knows everything. He wanted them to turn the shame that caused them to hide from Him into a contrite heart that turned back to Him in honesty and repentance. Shame that leads to repentance is a healthy shame that is released when the forgiveness is received.

But Adam and Eve did not choose to turn their shame into repentance; instead, they chose the path of contempt. Contempt is the energy of our shame which is directed toward someone with anger, someone who we feel is responsible for our sin and wounds. Contempt is a powerful feeling of angst against another. Adam and Eve blamed each other for their sin. When we choose the path of contempt, we are basically saying that our problem, sin, wound, or label must be someone's fault and that someone must pay. This type of contempt that is directed toward others interferes with our relationships and makes it hard for us to get along with others. We expect others to hurt us and find reasons not to enter into close, meaningful relationships, even with God. If we are rebellious against authority, loners, hard to get along with or critical, we are probably struggling with a deep contempt for others that comes out of shame. Community is impossible for us if we choose this route. We are destined to live in shallow relationships with others or in isolation.

Contempt changes if we see ourselves as the ultimate cause of our wounding. Self-contempt is the third way we may deal with our shame. Self-contempt interferes deeply with the positive identity which God gave to us. We blame ourselves for the bad things that have happened to us. The label that we wear is our own fault. Often abuse victims feel there must have been something about them that caused them to be chosen for the abuse. Deep inside is the feeling *it is my fault*. The end result of self-contempt is a self-hatred that shows itself in various ways. Depression, suicidal thought, self-mutilation, poor hygiene, passivity, and unhealthy lifestyle choices (such as drug or alcohol abuse or unprotected sexual activity) can all be linked to a self-contempt which comes out of shame.

We all have sin and wounds, so we must all learn to deal properly with shame. Shame that leads to repentance is the path to life. However, shame that leads to contempt is a detour away from life and ultimately leads us to hide. Some find it easier to hide than to repent. Hiding behind fig leaves and then behind trees was Adam and Eve's first response to their shame. The identity that arises out of our sin and wounds is not socially acceptable and it drives us to hide. No one enters a room and announces, *Hi, I'm Bob and I am a pervert!* We cannot be who we believe we are, so we must create another persona. The easiest way to hide is to find a way to present ourselves in public that is both believable and fairly easy to maintain. This public image or false self is a reaction to our shame (see False-self on the Life Chart).

The false self is like a mask that we choose to wear in order to keep others from knowing what we view as the *real truth* about us. Our choice of masks is based upon what we are familiar with, what works in our social settings, and what best fits our abilities and personalities. The athlete, the student, the religious zealot, the fixer, the control freak, the successful, the performer, the clown, and the know-it-all are all examples of the false self. The longer we wear the mask, the farther we get from the true self. Soon we find ourselves not only hiding from others but from ourselves and even from God. The freedom to live out of our heart is completely gone. Our hearts hold a dark secret that cannot be revealed. Our emotions are the keys to our heart and must also be closed down so that nothing of the secret is revealed. We cannot afford to feel because our feelings will take us back to the labels and lies. We are now forced to live out of our masks. People come to expect us to be smart, athletic, funny, or successful. We are bound to a certain role and the feel of the mask gets tighter and tighter. Ashamed of who we are, emotionally shut down, and living out of a mask, our life doesn't resemble the life for which we were created. Bondage, drudgery, and boredom all become words that describe our life, and the self-talk begins. There has to be more to life than *this*. And there is!

Carla was in one of my wife's Bible studies at church. As the ladies shared concerns and prayer requests, it became apparent that Carla was suffering from some severe exhaustion and was slipping into depression. As we began to uncover the root of the problem, we found that Carla, who was the mother of three elementary-aged children, was trying to work a part-time job, be a home-maker, and keep her kids involved in all of the extra-curricular activities that they desired. She took them to practices, served as team mom, room mother, and made snacks for every group. It seemed simple to suggest to Carla that she slow down her life. Even the mention of it was unthinkable for her. She was dependent on her performance as *super-mom* to feel good about herself. It was exhausting her, keeping her from celebrating her children, and trapping her in an endless cycle of *doing.* It was her identity and she could not change it.

The pain of wearing the mask and the bondage that it brings us seek relief. Added to the pain of the mask is the exhaustion that comes from performance. Our lives are not flowing freely out of our hearts; they are forced, performed, and hard to maintain. Self-medication becomes the only way to survive the pain and exhaustion of a suffocating mask. The medicine that we choose is a product of what appeals to us and what is a part of our lives at the time that the pain of wearing the mask becomes too great. Pornography, alcohol, drugs, work, money, possessions, sports, church, sexual exploits, travel, food, or relationships become the good feeling that allows us to forget briefly the pain of the mask (see Addictions on the Life Chart). The problem, of course, is that the addiction to these things contributes to the feeling of shame and fuels the cycle to continue at a more feverous pace. The weakness of giving in to the addiction reinforces our negative identity and binds us more deeply to the mask. We now enter in to a cycle of striving and indulging. We strive to prove that we are okay and live behind the mask. When that exhausts us we indulge ourselves in something that brings pleasure but also drives us to strive harder to prove that we are okay. Didn't Jesus promise rest? Does this sound like the life He came to offer, the life He died to give us? Does He really want us to just *grin and bear it* until all of our striving can cease?

At this point, any attempts on our part to reconnect with God without taking off the mask end up in religious performance. If we are not willing to be honest before the Lord, our relationship with Him is reduced to a system of religion where *doing* is all important and *being* is minimized. We cannot *be* in relationship with God because of our negative identity. We can only *do* things to appease Him and try to convince Him (and ourselves) that we are okay. Churches today are filled with people who are caught in this cycle, desiring life, desiring God, but powerless to get there because of our inability to take off the mask. The result is empty, powerless religion that ends up focused on judging others for what they are or aren't doing instead of enjoying life and inviting others into it. The good news of the Gospel has been reduced to a shallow bondage to rules and regulations.

The really good news is that you can choose life. We have established that because of Christ's death on the cross for us. Life is an every-moment possibility. The rest of this book will be about how to find yourself in the endless cycle and choose life at any point. Let's pause a moment and look at the Life Chart. Can you begin to see any way that you have detoured from life? As you keep the Life Chart in mind, let me share my story with you. Perhaps you will be able to relate.

Chapter 3—Questions to Ponder

1 Which of the four components of positive identity do you sense have been damaged in you?

2. What negative label have you placed on yourself? Why?

3. If shame is the sense that *there is something wrong with me*, do you struggle with shame?

4. Are you aware of any walls that you have erected around your emotions?

5. How would you describe your false self or mask?

6. Does your involvement with church help you to take off the mask? Why or why not?

7. In what ways do you tend to self-medicate from your pain? Do you consider these medications an addiction?

CHAPTER 4

My Story

⌒⌒⌒

I am adding this chapter for those of you who are reading this thinking, *Yeah, Bob, great theory.* The Life Chart presented in Chapter 3 did not come from a text book; it came from my life story. Several years after my recovery, I went on a series of retreats with some close brothers in the Lord. As we talked through our past, the beginnings of the chart were drawn up on a flip chart. Through the years that followed that retreat, I have gone deeper into how the chart and my life story mirror each other. So, with the chart fresh in your mind, let me share my story.

I guess I grew up like any other kid in the suburbs, looking for ways to enjoy life. I was riding bikes, building forts, swinging on the backyard swing set, playing ball, and swimming—anything to make me feel *alive.* I was passionate, active, and fully alive. As a youngster, though, my passion for life was suppressed. Very early I became acquainted with walls or boundaries that limited my ability to embrace life and experience it fully. An overly legalistic church and very restrictive parents kept me from venturing too far into life outside of our little world and instilled in me timidity in my approach to life. Their motivation was good and loving; the world was changing rapidly in the 60's and 70's, and there were many unfamiliar and sinful behaviors being promoted as legitimate. The fences that were built for me—far from the actual lines of right and wrong—did keep me from wandering into many areas of sin. But the timidity that grew out of my fear of breaking the rules kept me from embracing life fully and contributed to the secrecy that nearly destroyed me.

At an early age, I responded to an invitation at church to receive Christ as my Savior for the forgiveness of my sin. My decision was fairly utilitarian. I needed my sin forgiven in order to get to Heaven, and I was afraid of going to Hell. In spite of this, I did enjoy some times of spiritual life and growth as a child. I considered myself a Christian but really had no idea about a relationship with God. We went to church every Sunday and on Wednesday nights, and something about the system of that small world felt safe. I knew I was a sinner, since we were reminded of it every time we went to church. However, I had no idea what to do with the tremendous amount of guilt and shame that this sin brought. When I was forced by others to cross lines into what I considered *horrible* sins, I did not know how to handle the feelings.

I was about 10 years old when the name-calling began. I was slight of build, intelligent, uncoordinated, and musically inclined. The labels of *sissy, mamma's boy*, and *fag* were quickly attached to me by a group of older boys in the neighborhood. It has always been natural for bigger, stronger boys to bully those they see as weaker. This derisive verbal ridicule quickly escalated into physical abuse. Causing me physical pain, watching me cry, and reveling in my reactions to their torment became a favorite pastime of these boys. On one occasion, they knocked the wind out of me and then stood around and laughed when I couldn't catch my breath. On another, they led me to a bumble bee nest in the ground. They threw a rock and then ran while I stood there, ignorantly, and was stung multiple times. I can still hear their laughter. It wasn't long before some of the physical activity, fueled by their adolescent curiosity about sex, deteriorated into sexual abuse. I was held down and forced to perform sexual acts with them. I was younger and smaller than they were and the taunting about the size of my genitals and my smooth skin went deep into my mind. This was the final step in shutting me down spiritually and emotionally and the beginnings of my obsession with sex. I knew that these acts, outside of marriage and with the same sex, were wrong and perverted. Any mention of this kind of activity at church came with words like *Sodom and Gomorrah* and *abomination*. It would certainly not be safe to mention any of this at church.

To add to my shame for participating in these acts was the shame of knowing there was some pleasure involved. The pain of abuse would inevitably lead to the exhilaration of sexual release, something I had never before experienced. The combination of adrenalin from fear and hormones from sexual climax made an indelible mark on my young psyche. The Enemy began to articulate a lie that ran through my mind—*I must be at fault if I enjoyed any part of this*. The fear instilled in me about these kinds of sin and what happened to those people who indulged in them kept me from sharing anything with anyone at home or at church. I suffered in silence, letting the message of the wound sink deep into my soul. I was a pervert! I had moved out of the center position of the Life Chart and saw myself as a reflection of the sin and wounds. The label was pervert, and the lies built up a stronghold in me that would take years to tear down.

From that point on, I knew that there was something wrong with me. The deep sense of shame made me hate myself. Because of my timidity, I didn't have the courage to face my abusers or my own sin and turn to God in repentance. Instead, my shame became contempt, self-contempt in the form of self-hatred. I took every opportunity to put myself down and laugh at myself. I refused to engage in any activity in which I could not be the best. I shied away from anything athletic because my lack of coordination would be a clue to others revealing who I really was. The part of me I hated the most was my masculinity. I hated the *macho* in others; at the same time, I was drawn to the strength that it represented. I equated the perception of strength with a false definition of masculinity I knew I didn't have. Gender confusion had set in. I was so weak, I had given in, I had been dominated, and I was not a real man.

The gender confusion only increased my sense of shame. The shame of who I perceived myself to be is what motivated me to look for a way to hide. I was terrified that someone would figure out who I thought I was. Part of me, the true masculine part, simply withdrew. The other part decided that I would disguise my identity of pervert by being *perfect*. No one would be able to see past my perfect mask to the pervert within.

This mask of perfection evolved as I discovered ways that my flesh could compensate for the broken parts of my positive identity (virtue, community, power, and gender). Having lost all sense of value (virtue) in the depths of my shame, I tried to perform in perfect ways that would generate affirmation. I had to have straight A's in school, be the best son, the first chair in orchestra, and the teacher's pet. When I performed well in these roles, I felt good about myself for a while and was able temporarily to block out the shame. The problem with this mask, as with any mask, is that it had to be maintained. I could never rest. I always had to become better and better in order to keep the affirmations coming. I graduated from high school at 16 with nearly a 4.0. I then got married at 19, graduated from college and was ordained to the ministry at 20, and became a youth pastor at 21. I must be perfect . . . in school . . . at home . . . at church.

I presented myself as self-assured, self-confident and superior; but nothing could have been farther from the truth.

My sense of my power to choose had been completely destroyed by the acts of abuse. Repeatedly, I was overpowered by the strength of others who were bigger and stronger than I was. Regaining that sense of power required that I be in control of every situation in which I found myself. I manipulated the teacher into making me the teacher's pet, became the president of my youth group, planned family events, and bossed my friends around. Closely associated with this need to control was the need to belong to a community. Because of who I thought I was, I never felt like I fit in. My ticket into community was my ability to be in charge. Any group that I controlled became my community. They had to include me because I was in charge. That control was my way of showing strength; it was my masculinity. I had community, but it was forced and shallow. Deep inside I believed that if they knew who I really was, they would not include me at all. My career choice was motivated by this desire to be in control. Besides my family, the only other community that I had been involved in was church. The pastor was in charge at the church, so I was going to become a pastor.

The greatest part of my wounding was the damage done to my sexuality. I believed the lies and labels that others had placed on me and secretly harbored those thoughts as my identity for years. My secret fear was that I was gay. I hid my true masculinity and used my control to *feel* masculine and *look* masculine to others. As far as leadership was concerned, I was the man. Inside, though, I was confused about my sexuality. This confusion continued to fuel my shame in spite of the mask.

I believed the lies and labels that others had placed on me and secretly harbored those thoughts as my identity for years.

This cycle of shame and performance was an emotional roller coaster that was both exhausting and painful.

So now, shame had moved me from the right-hand side of the Life Chart to the left-hand side. I was now living in bondage to my mask of religious performance and control. I worked hard to prove that I was okay and to distance myself from the labels and lies that plagued my thinking. While it appeared to others that I really was that masked person, the thought of who I believed I really was never left me. I was a pervert, trying to come off as perfect.

In my pain, I sought relief. Self-medication is a natural coping mechanism for anyone in pain. What do we do when we have a headache? We look for the pain reliever. Emotionally and spiritually, we are no different. We look for something that will bring us pleasure, something that is available and works to reduce the pain. My medication was closely associated with my journey. Pornography, masturbation, and sexual fantasy provided an escape from the pain and pressure of the constant performance required in my role as pastor. However, it increased the sense of shame. Religious performance eased the pain of feeling like a pervert but led to exhaustion and further acting out. I entered a period of my life where I lived in the destructive cycle of striving and indulging. I worked hard to be the best and most caring pastor I could be. Then when exhausted or criticized, I indulged my flesh in pornography, masturbation, and sexual fantasy. The repetition of this cycle led to a deep depression.

The Enemy used depression to create a fog that would lead me down a path of despair. The truth became even harder to discern through the fog, and the lies increased in strength. The stronghold of lies and labels was so strong that the truth couldn't even penetrate it. I began to feel more and more that the wounded identity was the true me and that I would never overcome it. I begged God to take it away, but I never addressed what was driving it. I went forward at church invitations and retreat campfires and promised God over and over that I would never act out again, that I would be faithful. The repeated unanswered prayers and the repeated broken promises worked together to create a great disillusionment about God. Maybe it was all made up. Maybe God wasn't real. Maybe I was meant to be this way. Maybe He just didn't care. Maybe . . ..

The suicidal thoughts started very subtly; in the fog, I didn't even recognize them for what they were. I was tired and exhausted from the endless cycle of striving and indulging. I just wanted to go to sleep and never wake up. As this thought grew in my mind, I began to formulate a plan to make it happen. My double life had already taken its toll on me physically. I was experiencing high blood pressure, passing-out spells, and migraine headaches. No real medical cause was ever found for my symptoms, but the doctors were more than happy to medicate them. I started taking more and more of my medication to help me sleep and help me to forget my struggles.

Finally, the day came when I didn't care if I woke up or not. The thought that I kept repeating in my mind was that I wanted to go to sleep and never wake up. I had preached morning and evening messages at church the day before and felt emptier than I could ever remember. I went into my bedroom and began swallowing pills.

I don't even remember how far I got in the process when my wife came in. I fell apart in front of her. By the end of that day, just 24 hours after another religious performance, I was admitted to a psychiatric hospital and labeled suicidal. It was a humiliating experience. I was stripped of my belt, razor, shoe strings, and anything else that I might use to harm myself. I was put in a room where I could be watched so that I would not attempt suicide. I was heavily medicated. I lost my church, nearly lost my family, lost my perfect mask, and lost my capacity to maintain the façade of my past.

The psychiatric hospital was not the answer to all of my problems, but the Lord did use it to provide me with a safe place to let down my guard and share with my wife and others what was really going on inside of me. Wouldn't it have been awesome if the church had been that safe place? HONESTY—this was my first choice toward life. Maybe it will help you make this choice as well.

When my journey was held inside in secrecy, it had great power over me. I felt like I was the only one who experienced these things or felt this way. Since sharing my journey with others, I have come to understand that we all have a story. Some involve much more pain than mine and some less. We *all* have a story and we *all* need to choose life.

The next 10 chapters will introduce 10 choices that we can make that will lead us back into the center of the Life Chart, back to life. These choices are all every-moment possibilities for everyone who has received Christ by faith because of the gift of choice God created us with and because of the life that Jesus came to offer. They are not necessarily presented in any order that must be followed. They are not one-time decisions that assure us of living in the center of the Life Chart and fully embracing life every day. They are choices that must be made daily because we tend to allow our journey, sin, wounds, flesh, coping mechanisms, culture, the lies of the Enemy, and any other factor to move us away from life. It is my prayer that we will choose life in any situation where we find ourselves feeling distant from God, disconnected from His voice, living in shame, or living in bondage.

Chapter 4—Questions to Ponder

After reading Bob's story, do you see how sin and wounds drive us away from
life?

Briefly write your own story. Identify the sin and wounds that separated you
from the Father, the lies and labels you believe about yourself, the feelings
of shame, the masks, and the self-medications. Include also your involvement in the cycle of striving and indulging.

Choose Honesty

⤮

*An acknowledgement and confession of all of the ways that I try
to make life work apart from Christ frees me from the lies that
keep me stuck and creates a teachable spirit within me.*

As we have worked through the Life Chart and walked together through my own journey, we probably feel affirmed in our initial reason for picking up this book. We are missing the life that God intended for us. So, how do we get there? How do we choose life? Where do we begin? It is time for us to get honest with ourselves and with God about what is really going on in our lives. It is time to confess. You have probably heard the statement that confession is good for the soul. The concept is biblical. Scripture tells us that confession leads to forgiveness[41] and healing.[42]

What is confession? The biblical word literally means to *speak the same.* Confession is taking my behavior and lining it up with God's standard, fully admitting that I have fallen short.[43] Confession is telling my story, with all of its detours, sins, wounds, masks, and addictions, leaving out nothing; i.e., the whole truth. It is taking all of the cards that we hold in our hands, some tightly to our chest, and laying them all down on the table before God—fully exposed.

But Bob isn't that risky? Do I have to air all of my dirty laundry for everyone to see in order to experience the life for which I was created? I am not recommending that you write a book so that everyone can read about your sordid past. Confession is risky; but the risk is determined not by what we share but with whom we share it. I want to encourage you to take the first steps on this journey toward your true self, toward life, by confessing honestly to yourself and to God. The risk in getting honest with self is that it will bring up all of the emotions that we have tried to keep inside for so long and will force us to deal with

the issues that we have tried to keep locked away. Confession to God holds no risk at all; He already knows what is really going on in our lives. He just wants to hear us admit it, to own it. When God asks questions, it isn't to get information, it is to challenge us to own the information. Remember Adam in the Garden of Eden? God asked, "Where are you Adam?" He didn't ask so that Adam would reveal his whereabouts; He asked so that Adam would admit what he had done.

Confession is telling my story, with all of its detours, sins, wounds, masks, and addictions, leaving out nothing.

Why choose honesty? Why confess? In the Bible, sin is likened to darkness, while life in Christ is light. As believers, we have the privilege of walking in the light. If we say we are children of the light, and continue to walk in darkness, we are called liars. Our behavior is inconsistent with our professed identity. The admonition to those who are walking in darkness is to confess.[44] Sin grows as we continue to keep it hidden. In the darkness of secrecy, there is no power to overcome, no encouragement to relinquish, and no accountability to move us forward. Addiction and sin grow stronger in the dark.

Consider the example of David. At a time when the kings went to war, he stayed home and indulged himself by looking upon Bathsheba as she bathed on the rooftop of her house. He chose to give in to his lust and committed adultery with her. After his detour into adultery, he made a conscious choice to cover up his sin, choosing to keep it hidden in the darkness. He did not choose honesty. In order to keep his sin covered up, he was forced to ensure the death of Bathsheba's husband (murder!) and live a lie to all in his household. His decision *not* to choose honesty was a choice to allow sin to remain in the dark and grow stronger, leading to even more sin. David never experienced any healing from this situation until he chose to be honest with the prophet Nathan who confronted him.[45]

I personally struggled with my sexual addiction in the dark for over 20 years. I would confess my individual choices to give in to my lust and make all kinds of promises to God about my behaviors. I would draw lines and promise never to cross them. However, I never admitted to myself or to God all that was going on in my life. I never connected the dots between my religious performance, my past abuse, my self-contempt, and the sexual acting out. Because I refused to bring my sin fully into the light, the desire and power of the sin grew stronger, and I found myself crossing every line that I had vowed not to cross.

> *Sin grows as we continue to keep it hidden.*

Vows of the will made in the darkness are impotent. Since our sin grows in the dark, the longer we remain silent, the more speed we pick up before we hit the wall and the more devastation that is caused. We tell ourselves that we cannot confess because it would hurt too much and hurt too many people. What we don't realize is that the longer it remains hidden, the greater the hurt.

How do we begin? Confession begins with a humble admission that we are needy, that we don't have it all together, and we can't seem to make our lives work on our own. Neediness is not a sin, and it is not a weakness. When God created man and placed him in the Garden of Eden, he said it was not good for him to be alone. Adam, even before his choice to sin, had needs that were not being met. He had a beautiful place to live, provision for food, a job to do, and a relationship with God. But he still had needs. How much more, with the taint of sin in our flesh, do we have needs? We need life but we are looking for it in all of the wrong places (sound familiar?). Instead of confessing our neediness to God and allowing Him to come in and meet our needs, we choose to believe that we can meet our own needs, or we can make life work on our own. This choice—the choice *not* to be honest—costs us and increases our neediness. We are using our neediness to draw us into sin, independence and self-effort instead of using it to draw us into meaningful relationships with God and others.

I needed to know that I was okay and I was not a pervert. I needed to know that others accepted me. I needed to be affirmed in my masculinity. All these were legitimate needs, but I chose to handle them in the wrong way because I refused openly to acknowledge them as needs. For part of my journey, I simply denied that I had these needs. I couldn't even admit them to myself. I clung to my religious mask and pretended I was okay. I compared myself with others who were outwardly more messed up than I was, and that helped me to feel better about myself. Unfortunately, denial only increases the intensity of the feeling of neediness. When I could no longer deny that I had needs that weren't being met, I turned to avoiding those needs. I came up with coping mechanisms that would bring some relief without really addressing the root of the need. I began to seek the praise of men to satisfy my need for acceptance. The problem with this approach is that there is no way you can please everyone. You will die trying, and I almost did. The effort required to try to please others definitely contributed to the exhaustion that fueled my thoughts of suicide. I also began to use control as a means to exert masculinity. I did not have a good sense of the true masculine because of my past. So I chose control as a way to show that I was masculine. *Bob in charge* was the false masculine coping mechanism that I chose to help me avoid my real need. Unfortunately, this control kept me from submitting to God and caused pain in many others around me. When my coping mechanisms not only failed but left me tired and disillusioned, I turned to pacifying my needs. It didn't matter where the good feelings came from; I just wanted to feel good. My sexual addiction provided momentary pleasure, so more and more, I turned to it for relief from the gnawing needs in my spirit. The needs for intimacy, relationship, and masculinity were temporarily met in the shallowness of sexual activity. Of course, this approach also made me feel even needier after the pleasure of the moment was gone.

We all have needs. We need acceptance. We need affirmation. We need to be loved. We need to feel secure and significant. We can try denying these needs, avoiding them through coping mechanisms or pacifying them through pleasure, but we always end up right back where we started—needy. The only way out is to choose honesty, to confess freely the fullness of our neediness to ourselves and to God.

Looking back, it would have been so much easier just to admit my neediness to God and ask Him to meet my needs. Confession would have saved me many years of heartache. Why is confession so hard for us? It is because we believe the lies. At the top of the list of lies is the belief that if we admit the problem to ourselves fully, it will empower the problem to get worse. If we pretend it doesn't exist, it cannot take over our lives. If we just would spend a moment thinking about this logic, we would easily see its shallowness. Pretending that an enemy army is not camped outside of our walls will not cause the enemy to leave or help us win the battle. Seeing the enemy, identifying the enemy, talking about the enemy, soliciting help against the enemy and engaging the enemy is the only way to victory. Lie number one is exposed!

The second lie that makes it hard for us to admit our neediness is that we feel if we open up our feelings, the pain will be unbearable. We use words like:

I am afraid I will lose it.
I am afraid I will fall apart.
I will not be able to handle it.

The feeling I carried around for years, the feeling that scared me to death, that feeling that stayed in the dark was, *I am gay.* My first sexual experiences were with males. There must have been something about me that caused this to happen. On top of this, the first experiences of sexual release brought some pleasure. *How could I enjoy something like that? I must be gay.* This feeling was buried deep for a long time. I could not allow myself even to form the words. If I let out this feeling, I would not be able to bear the shame. I would fall apart; I would lose it. The truth was that keeping this feeling inside is what caused me to fall apart. When I was in the psychiatric hospital, I was finally able to say the words out loud and express my greatest fear. I felt relief, as if some pent-up pressure had been released. The problem was out in the open, the cards were on the table, and now we could begin to sort through them all. Yes, there will be tremendous emotion associated with confession. Yes, it may hurt to face the feelings and events from the past. But you will not fall apart; you will not lose it. In fact, you will feel a little lighter. Confession takes us out of the darkness and into the light where the healing presence of the Father awaits us. Lie number two is disproved!

The third lie that keeps us from admitting our neediness concerns our identity. In the first chapters of this book, we learned that because of our sin, wounds, and shame, we have taken on a false identity—the false self—a negative identity. This false identity grows out of our neediness. If we admit our neediness, we have to lay down this identity. While we hate the mask, it is all we know. We have come to believe it is who we are. We have become comfortable behind the mask. The fear of laying down this identity and possibly not knowing who we are is great and keeps us from admitting our neediness. We know that we will have to lay down our false identity if we remove its foundation.

Some time after leaving the hospital, it became clear that I should no longer serve in the role of pastor. I needed to lay this false identity down. I struggled with this for a long time. Although the identity of pastor was wearing me out, it was all I knew. I was hesitant to give it up. When I finally did lay it down, I floundered for a while. In order to feed my family, I delivered newspapers, drove a truck, did courier work, and tutored struggling students. Who was I in all of this? I remember one morning about 5:00 as I drove up and down the streets throwing newspapers, a lady emerged from her house in her bathrobe screaming choice words at me because I had frequently thrown her paper into the bushes. She had waited for me on this morning to give me a piece of her mind. As I listened to her tirade, I thought to myself, w*hom does she think she is talking to?* The answer that came immediately to my mind was *the paperboy.* As a family man in my late 30's who had led a congregation, this was a sobering moment. I could no longer lean on my profession as my identity. With no false mask to wear, the passion to learn who I really was became stronger. It drove me to the truth of God's word and into a recovery program that affirmed who I really was in Christ. Laying down the false identity is difficult, but it is not the end. It is the beginning of walking in your true identity in Christ. We will cover this topic later.

There is one more thing that keeps us from choosing honesty. We come to face it through another of God's questions, spoken through Jesus to the man who had been lying paralyzed by the pool of Bethesda for 38 years. The question is, "Do you want to be whole?" Part of choosing honesty is coming to terms with the fact that we truly are tired of the

Do you want to be whole? | way our life is not working and we want to be whole. The truth is, though, not everyone wants to be whole. Consider the words of Mark Buchanan's book, *The Rest of God*, in the chapter on "Restore."

> "A curious thing about restoration is that it doesn't need doing. Strictly speaking, life carries on without it. Restoration is an invasion of sorts. It's fixing something that's broken, but broken so long it's almost mended. This man (at the pool) had already adapted to his misfortunes, made all the necessary adjustments. Restoration meddles with what he'd learned to handle, removes what he'd learned to live with, bestows what he'd learned to live without. Replacements have been found already, thank you all the same.
>
> "These people are doing fine just the way they are. They've learned to live this way. They've almost accepted it. They've taught them-

selves tricks to bypass it, to contain it. To utilize it, even. They've built lives around not being whole. They've learned, if not to welcome, at least not to spurn those things their sickness drags in with it. They've learned not to mourn the absence of those things it chases away. Secretly, perhaps, they have come to love their illness."[46]

This last point is one that we may be quick to pass over. Of course we want to be whole. Perhaps it would be good for us to pause here for a moment and think of all the ways we have become accustomed to our lives and how difficult any change would be for us. Do we truly want to be whole?

The relief that comes with confession is confirmed by David. He describes the time that he hid his sin of adultery as a time of drought, groaning, heaviness, and weakness. He contrasts this with the happiness and blessings that he experienced when he confessed.[47] My own experience with keeping the sin in the darkness was also characterized by weakness and drought. I developed migraines, high blood pressure, anxiety, and depression. It was the medications for these, the symptoms of my real problem, which I used to try to end it all.

Choosing life begins when we choose honesty; being honest with ourselves, God and others. Admitting our neediness to ourselves is the first step. It brings clarity to where we really are in our journey. Admitting our neediness to God is the only way to receive the grace, forgiveness, and truth that God offers. These topics will be covered in Chapters 6-8. Admitting our need to others creates a sense of authentic community that both encourages us and holds us accountable. This will be covered in Chapter 11.

Begin by journaling. Use Diagram 3 to identify the detours you have taken. What sin or wound causes the deepest sense of shame in you? What lies have you believed about yourself? What labels do you wear that you don't want anyone to know? How have you internalized your shame? What coping mechanisms has contempt fostered in your life? What mask do you wear in order to prove to others that you are acceptable? What addictions have you developed to help ease the pain of your inner struggles? What has kept you from choosing honesty up to this point? Do you really want to be whole? How have you tended to rationalize your struggles? Answering these questions openly and honestly with yourself on paper will begin to move you in the right direction. See Questions to Ponder at the end of this chapter.

Next, find a quiet place where you can be alone with God. You may want to use some symbol of His presence, since sensing His presence in the midst of the struggle is always difficult. Use a cross, a Bible, a picture, or some part of nature that reminds you of His presence. As you sit quietly in His presence, just begin to talk aloud to Him about where you find yourself on Diagram 3. Admit to the Father verbally the sin, wounds, lies, labels, shame, contempt, masks, and addictions. Allow anger to surface. Allow shame to be exposed. Allow yourself to feel the pain of this place, acknowledging at each point that Christ's death on the cross pays the price.

Now read the next three chapters on grace, forgiveness, and truth. You are not fully prepared to receive these wonderful gifts from God until you have confessed your neediness to Him. Don't allow yourself continually to wallow in this place of confession at the foot of the cross. There is a balance here. Not having a time of confession makes it impossible to move on. Too much time in confession keeps you stuck at the cross, unable to move into intimate relationship with the Father.

Begin to pray that the Lord would bring someone into your life with whom you can be honest and open about your journey. Finding and connecting to a community of support and encouragement will be covered in Chapter 11.

Since God created us for life, and since Christ came to bring life, these choices for life will be honored by the Father. You are choosing life and He is ready and willing to live through you.

Chapter 5—Questions to Ponder

While most of these questions will have been answered in your story from Chapter 4's questions, make a statement about each of the following that would be parallel to what God would say about each one. For example: *I have been abandoned by those who were supposed to love me and I have responded by living a life of anger and self-focus.*

Confess your sin and wounds.

Confess the lies you have believed about yourself.

Confess the labels you have worn as identity.

Confess the coping mechanisms you have developed to deal with life.

Confess the masks that you wear to hide behind.

Confess the sinful ways you have self-medicated.

CHAPTER 6

Choose Grace

Receiving God's grace through Christ's sacrifice frees me from the labor of self-effort (flesh) and leads me to choose Christ as life.

Doesn't confession feel like a cleansing shower? Doesn't it feel good to get all of that out? Choosing honesty has freed us from the illusion that we can make life work on our own, and with the illusion goes the pressure. We don't have to make life work on our own. Having laid down our own ways, we are now ready to choose God's way. We are now ready to choose grace.

Grace is defined in many ways. Some use an acronym and define it as *God's Riches at Christ's Expense*. Others simply say that it is unmerited favor. The truth is that in its broadest sense, grace is God's operating system. Because of who He is (holy) and who we are (sinful), there was no way for us to get to God and no reason for God to reach out to us. The fact that He did reach out to us, in a most dramatic way through Christ, is grace (unprompted, unearned love). It is the only way that God allows us to have a relationship with Him.

You have chosen honesty—now what? The danger of being in this place on your journey is that—having confessed your neediness and the inadequacy of your old ways of dealing with life—you will simply *try* something else, some new system. Trying implies works, and works preclude grace. You cannot *try* anything to guarantee the life that God desires for you to experience. You can only receive it. He has already accomplished all we need, and it only comes by way of grace. Our restoration to life is fully dependent on the grace of God. It is not dependent on any change of behavior on our part, any penance that we can do, or any disciplines that we can maintain. We must allow confession at the foot of the cross to lead us to receive relationship with God by grace.

Journey back with me to the Garden again. Adam and Eve have just chosen death instead of life by eating of the forbidden fruit. The punishment has been foretold and must be executed. They must die. The next event is unscripted, unpredicted, and unprovoked. God, in an act of utter grace, covers their sin and shame with the sacrifice of an animal and continues to dialogue with them. Sure there were consequences. They were removed from the Garden, their bodies began to deteriorate toward death, and their relationship with God was limited. God still extended grace. Not only did he temporarily cover their sin and shame, but He made a promise to them that one day, the "seed of the woman" would forever deal with the evil one and his sin.[48] Grace. What had they done to deserve this second chance? Nothing. It was all God's doing, not dependent on them at all. It was grace.

Our restoration to life is fully dependent on the grace of God.

Traveling forward on the biblical timeline, we return to the story of David, a man after God's own heart. He had sat with God, heard from God, and was given great blessings from God. But, as we have seen, David chose to commit adultery with Bathsheba and then chose to cover his sin instead of choosing honesty. When he was finally confronted by the prophet Nathan, he knew that the punishment was death. Again, the next part of Nathan's pronouncement was unexpected and unforeseen. The Lord had put away David's sin. Certainly there were consequences that worked themselves out in his family, but God extended grace to David by letting him live and letting him continue to rule over His people.[49] What had David done to deserve this second chance? Nothing. It was all God's doing, not dependent on him at all. It was grace.

Grace comes to us in the same way—unscripted, unexpected, and undeserved. At our lowest point, believing there is nothing salvageable in our lives, the Father extends His grace to us through the forgiveness offered by Jesus. I remember on my own journey being completely caught off guard by His grace. Confession had taken me to the lowest place yet. I had admitted my sin and wounds for the first time, and it was painful. I had spent the first few days in the psychiatric hospital on suicide watch because of my depression and demeanor. The door to my room was kept slightly ajar and someone checked on me every 30 minutes. My belt, shoestrings, and razor had been taken from me so that I could not easily hurt myself. In the middle of the night, the Father called to me, and I was drawn to His Word for the first time since I arrived at the hospital. My wife had brought a small Bible to me, one that had been given to me by my youth group on my 30th birthday. I crept out of my room into the light of the hallway, sat on the floor, and began to read the Psalms. There is a word in the Psalms that is translated as love, loving kindness, and mercy. It is the Hebrew word *chesed,* and it communicates the grace of God clearer than any other Old Testament Word. I read through the Psalms that night and marked every occurrence of that word that I could find. As the impact of His grace began to settle on me, the tears began to come, and I literally collapsed into the arms of the Savior. I knew that I could not make my life better. I feared that it never would get better. I knew that I did not deserve for it to be better. In spite of all of this, He extended His grace toward me and I, having exhausted every other avenue, simply chose it. What had I done to deserve this second chance? Nothing. It was all God's doing, not dependent on me at all. It was grace.

I cannot say that self-effort did not creep back into my recovery process. Each time I began to *lean on my own understanding,*[50] He gently reminded me that grace was the only operating system He uses. One of my old strategies was to try to bargain with God. I would promise Him something if He would take away this desire or give me victory over this temptation. Bargaining is not part of God's operating system.

I am reminded of the story of Leroy. It was Leroy's birthday and he wanted a red bicycle. So he boldly approached his mother with his request. She was not nearly as convinced that this was a good idea. She reminded him that he had not been particularly good this past year and she wasn't sure that he deserved a new red bike. She suggested that he go upstairs and write a short note to God explaining why he felt that he deserved a red bicycle. Leroy went trudging up the steps, got out his paper and pencil and defiantly wrote:

Dear God,
    I have been a very good boy this year and I think I
    deserve a red bicycle.
                        Signed, Leroy.

After reading what he had written, it slowly dawned on him that while he may be able to fool his mother, God was another story. He surely would not buy this approach. So, Leroy tore up his letter and wrote another. Perhaps a less aggressive approach would be better.

> Dear God,
>> I have tried to be a good boy this year and I would like it
>> if you would allow me to have a red bicycle.
>> Signed, Leroy.

He felt a little better about this note but as he reflected, his heart sank. He knew it was not true. He had not really tried to be good, and God knew it. He sat down and began to think. Finally, he had an idea. He went downstairs and asked his mother if he could go down the street to the church. His mother was pleased; she thought perhaps this little exercise was moving in the right direction. Leroy entered the church and went straight to the front of the sanctuary where a small nativity scene was settled on the communion table. After standing there hesitating for a few moments, he quickly grabbed the small statue of Mary, shoved it in his pocket, and ran back to his bedroom. Once the door was closed, he got out paper and pencil and began to write:

> Dear God,
>> I've got your mama. If you ever want to see her again, give me a
>> red bicycle for my birthday.
>> Signed, Leroy.

When we are confronted with the reality of our condition and brutally honest about our detours and our poor choices, it does seem that our only hope is to try to bargain with God by doing some good works, making some big promises, getting into an accountability group, or becoming more rigorous in our religious performance. Nothing could be farther from the truth. It is in this place, the place where we have confessed our sin and wounds and that we have nothing to offer Him where He offers us His grace. It is up to us to receive it.

The trouble is that all of our religious training has taught us to believe otherwise. Brennan Manning says, "For many people in the church, Christianity is not Good News. The Gospel is not glad tidings of freedom and salvation proclaimed by Christ Jesus, but a rigid code of *dos* and *don'ts*, a tedious moralizing, a list of minimum requirements for avoiding the pains of Hell."[51] Didn't Jesus come to bring life? The church has the same response that the religious leaders had in Jesus' day. It is afraid that with the dangerous freedom of the grace of God, the systems developed by the church will lose their place. Let us pray that they do! We don't need a religious system, we need a Savior.

Can you see then how choosing grace will stop the never-ending cycle of striving and indulging? We spend all of our time trying to eliminate the ways that we indulge ourselves with the pleasures of sin (alcohol, drugs, food, money, shopping, gambling, sex, etc.). But the best way to end the cycle is to choose the grace of God so that we can stop striving, since the striving actually fuels our indulging. Relationship with God is not about striving. Jesus invites us to rest, not strive, because He did all of the striving for us and won the victory that we could never win.

> *We don't need a religious system, we need a Savior.*

Sam struggled with a drinking problem. As he moved into recovery, he had no problem with choosing honesty. He was devastated by his poor choices and more than willing to wallow in them at the foot of the cross. Choosing grace, though, was a different story. "Bob, I need to understand why I keep doing this!" I would assure him that while knowing the drivers behind his drinking may help him in his recovery, it was not necessary for him to understand it all in order to enter into relationship with God. "Then tell me what to do. Anything, I'll do it. Should I go to rehab? Should I get another sponsor? Should I confess in front of the church? Should I join an accountability group?" Again, I assured him that some of these things may indeed prove helpful on his journey, but that none of them were necessary to enter into a relationship with God. "But I can't have a relationship with God and drink like this," he would argue. I encouraged Sam to bring his drinking into the presence of God, allow the grace of God to accept him just the way he was, alcohol and all, and then trust God for the rest. Sam felt that he had to stop drinking before he could enter into a meaningful relationship with God. Sam was drinking because he saw himself as a drunk. If he could choose grace and step into the presence of God in spite of the drinking, he could become new, receive a new identity, and then have the power to live in that new identity. But, even if he chose to continue to drink, he would still be a child of God. This proved more than Sam could wrap his mind around.

The stumbling block that kept Sam from moving forward is the same one that blocked my progress for years. I couldn't embrace a relationship with God because I believed I was a pervert. I had to clean up my act first and then go to the Father. In order to participate in my sin, I had to exclude God and live a double life. Understanding grace allowed me to bring my sin and wounds into His presence and there receive grace for it all.

What will the grace of God do for us if we receive it? It will do the one thing that we have been longing for all of our life: it will make us accepted by God. Ephesians 1:6 in the King James Version says that we are ". . . accepted in the beloved." The Greek word that is used here is the same word that is used by the Angel Gabriel when he addressed Mary to announce that she was carrying the holy child. Gabriel says, "Rejoice, highly favored one!"[52] We are the "highly favored ones" of God! We are accepted by the God of the universe, not because of what we have done, but because of what He has done for us.

Our sin and wounds have made us feel unacceptable to God. We have been striving for too long to prove that we are acceptable by the masks we wear. Through grace, God is offering a better way. Lewis Smedes in his book, *Shame and Grace*, says, "Grace is the beginning of our healing because it offers the one thing we need most: to be accepted without regard to whether we are acceptable. Grace stands for a gift; it is the gift of being accepted before we become acceptable."[53] Since grace is a gift, it only remains that we receive the gift.

Grace stands for a gift; it is the gift of being accepted before we become acceptable.

How do we receive this grace? Receive Jesus. Paul told Titus that God's grace had made an appearance to all men.[54] Grace had taken on a visible form, the form of Jesus. His sacrifice on the cross for us forever settles the question of our acceptability. All sin and wounds are erased, guilt and shame are overcome, and even death is conquered. When we, by faith, receive Jesus, we receive the grace of God and are accepted by Him. No more striving, no more trying, no more religious systems. Rest.[55]

Receiving Jesus is more than praying a *sinner's prayer* to escape eternity in Hell. It is inviting Jesus to take away everything that separates us from the Father, believing that His sacrifice was for us, restoring us to relationship with the Father. It is inviting the life and power of Christ to come into our lives and be our source, identity, and hope. It is asking Him to take away our heart of sin and give us a new heart, a good heart, from which we can live freely. It is changing our identity from a sinner to a saint. It is a new birth! The decisions that follow of choosing forgiveness, truth, etc., will not be possible apart from choosing Jesus and His grace. When we choose grace, we choose to allow Christ to live in us and be our life. We no longer need to find life in anything else. With Christ in us, as our life, the choices for life begin to flow. Choose grace! Choose life!

Chapter 6—Questions to Ponder

1. Take a moment to reflect upon God's grace. Write out a definition of grace in your own words.

2. Describe some of the ways that you have tried to resolve your problems apart from grace (striving).

3. Reflect on your own journey and record here some of the significant encounters that you have had with God's grace.

4. How is bargaining with God contrary to grace? In what ways have you tried to bargain with God in the past?

5. Explain in your own words why a "religious system" is not what you need. How has a system let you down in the past?

6. Complete the following statement with several things that you learned from this lesson: Because of God's grace, I am . . .

CHAPTER 7

Choose Forgiveness

❦

*Receiving God's complete forgiveness and extending it frees me
from the bondage of sin and wounds.*

At this point in my healing process, I was beginning to feel like the spin cycle of depression and addiction was slowing down. Clarity and direction were giving the feeling of forward motion on the journey toward healing. I felt free, at least freer than I had ever felt before. This feeling was such a relief from the years of turmoil that I found myself beginning to relax. This was both positive and negative. The positive side was I was no longer obsessed with my struggles and beginning to experience and celebrate other parts of my life. The negative aspect was this new experience diminished my passion to keep moving forward. I share this with you as a warning; don't stop now. Do not allow satisfaction with the progress made lead to complacency and deter you from the next life choice—the choice for forgiveness. This decision is absolutely vital to continuing your progress toward life. Let me explain.

Imagine that you come upon an open field and discover a hot air balloon. The basket is sitting upright on the grass, and the fabric of the balloon is lying off to the side in a heap. There is no life to it. Eventually, someone comes along and ignites the gas burner, filling the balloon with heated air. As the balloon inflates to its full expanse, it begins to rise, lifting the basket off the ground. You leap into the basket and your pulse quickens as the balloon gains altitude. You eagerly anticipate floating lazily above the fields and hills. You feel free! You are caught off guard and startled when the balloon abruptly stops its upward climb, throwing you to the floor of the basket. You scramble to your feet and look over the side of the basket to see why you have stopped. The anchor ropes are still tied to the basket and are tethering it to the ground. Unless these ropes are released, you will rise no farther. In the same way, not receiving God's complete forgiveness and release from our sin or not releasing completely those who have wounded us, will keep us from moving forward on this healing journey toward life. We are still tethered to the ground of the past by the ropes of unforgiveness, and freedom is impossible.

What is forgiveness? The biblical word literally means to *leave* or *let go*. It is as if we are holding on to (tied down to) an offense from the past and still expecting some retribution. We are either holding on to the feeling there is some penance we must do in order to make it right, or we are tied to the feeling there is something someone *owes* us. Either way, the offense is unresolved and we remain in bondage to it, held back from moving forward into life.

Forgiveness releases us from that bondage by embracing that full resolution of the offense has occurred at the cross of Jesus.

In fact, we are not only in bondage to the offense itself and all of its pain, we are also in bondage to the emotions attached to the offense (anger, humiliation, fear), as well as any lies that are attached to the offense (*I am such a loser; I am so inadequate; I am so stupid*). Forgiveness releases us from that bondage by embracing that full resolution of the offense has occurred at the cross of Jesus.

Jesus taught on forgiveness by telling a parable in Matthew 18:21-35. In the story, a king looked through his books and noticed a very large unpaid debt. He approached the man who owed the money, and finding that he did not have the money to pay, ordered him to debtor's prison until the debt was satisfied. The man begged for mercy, and the king decided to totally release him from the debt. He didn't have to pay it later. He didn't have to justify why it wasn't paid. He didn't have to pay a portion of it. He didn't have to perform any particular service in return. He wasn't put on a payment plan. The king simply released him from the debt. This is forgiveness. The debtor did not deserve forgiveness of the debt, and he could not earn forgiveness of the debt. Forgiveness has its source in the one doing the forgiving and is not dependent on the one needing forgiveness. Forgiveness is a grace offered that can only be received. Scripture tells us that when the sinless Son of God went to the cross, He took all of our sin and "cancelled out the certificate of debt"[56] that was against us. You could say "paid in full." Scripture also tells us that He removes our sin "as far as the east is from the west"[57] and that he will "remember our sins no more."[58] It is clear that when God forgives us, he releases it—completely. Let's just pause here a moment and let that sink in. We are released from every bad thing we have ever thought or done. He doesn't hold any of it against us. He does not expect any retribution. He does not expect us to do any penance. He does not let our past sin disqualify us from relationship or service to Him. We are forgiven. The debt is paid in full. (Feel free to have a private praise session here.)

Sure, you may respond that is "easy for Him to do; He's God, but I am not a forgiving person." The truth is, if you have received Jesus by grace, you have received Him as your life and He is a forgiving person. You may not have been a forgiving person in the past or may even have a history of holding grudges, but now you are a forgiving person. For this reason, God can boldly command us to "forgiv[e] each other, just as in Christ God forgave you."[59] The forgiveness that we extend to others is *exactly* the same as the forgiveness that we get from God. We can forgive in this way because Christ lives in us.

Forgiveness must begin with receiving. The verse quoted above from Ephesians 4 reveals that the forgiveness we extend to others has a precedent in, and flows out of, the forgiveness we have received. If we choose not to receive God's forgiveness for our past, we maintain our shame and guilt, crippling our ability to grow in our relationship with Him. We feel guilt for what we have done, and we feel shame for who we perceive ourselves to be. We will deal with shame more in Chapter 9. The combination of these feelings leads us further from our true self. Since we can't seem to rid ourselves of this guilt and shame, we are motivated to cover them up which leads us to live from behind a mask out of a false self. The guilt and shame over our past sins also causes us to strive to be acceptable to God. We are drawn to legalistic religious systems that have no power to change us from the inside out. Our striving doesn't free us but leads us to more sin through indulging. Living in the power of the true self requires complete freedom from our own offenses (sins) and the offenses of others (wounds). If our desire is to choose life, we must choose forgiveness.

To put it simply, if we have any feeling that we must pay for our past wrongs or harbor the belief that others "owe" us for the wrongs they have committed against us, then we are not free to live the life for which God created us. We are still attached to events, feelings, and lies that cause the detours from life as we talked about in Chapter 3. These detours lead us to live a life of contempt and isolation instead of love and community. In his book, *Addiction and Grace*, Gerald May reveals the connection between forgiveness and the true freedom to love ourselves and others. He writes,

> "Sin, then, is not just ignorance or moral straying, but a kind of bondage or slavery from which one must be delivered into freedom. Freedom is possible through a mysterious, incarnational synthesis of human intention and divine grace. The issue is not simply whether one follows personal attachments or follows God. It is instead a question of aligning one's intention with the God within us and with us, through love and in grace. To make the alignment possible, Jesus proclaimed a message of radical forgiveness, not only forgiveness of humanity by God, but also forgiveness of one another by people. In this radical forgiveness, it is even possible to be freed of attachment to one's own guilt for or justification of the wounds one has inflicted upon others. True love of self, a reverence for the essential goodness of God's creation, is made possible. Herein lies the potential for endless freedom in the service of love. Nothing, not even one's own sinfulness, has to remain as an obstacle to the two greatest commandments."[60]

When May speaks of this freedom being made possible by a synthesis of human intention (choice) and divine grace (forgiveness), he is echoing the sentiment of this chapter—choose forgiveness.

If forgiveness is so vital to our experience of the life of grace, and it is abundantly available, because of Christ's work on the cross, why is it that we find it so hard to forgive? Perhaps if we name the roadblocks that keep us from choosing forgiveness, the obstacles can be removed and we can move toward this great release into freedom. Let's name and jump these hurdles together. Honestly evaluate the list below and identify which tend to keep you from moving toward forgiveness. Then claim the corresponding truth.

Pride—forgiving someone makes me look weak. I want to feel better than others. I want to be strong and superior. I'm right and I don't want to give in.

> **Truth**—*Pride is what keeps me in bondage and hinders my growth.*

I don't want to give up my excuse-making system. It is my way of coping with life.

> **Truth**—*I can learn a whole new way of living if I forgive.*

I want to be able to feel in control and manipulate others by holding their offense over them.

> **Truth**—*I am really the one out of control and in bondage when I don't forgive.*

If I forgive, I may get hurt again.

> **Truth**—*I am going to get hurt again whether I forgive or not. Dealing with the hurt frees me from its bondage and enables me to react differently to further wounds.*

If I ignore it, the problem will go away.

> **Truth**—*It may get buried for a while but it will resurface.*

The persons who wronged me need to pay for it. They need to learn a lesson.

> **Truth**—*Vengeance belongs to God; I am not their judge.*

I am a failure in understanding God's love and forgiveness for me.

> **Truth**—*You cannot give what you do not possess. Receive God's forgiveness.*

It seems too easy and feels like I am condoning their sin.

> **Truth**—*The fact is that in forgiveness we actually fully charge the debt to them and then release it, recognizing that it took the blood of Christ to forgive it. The sin is not minimized.*

I am waiting for the person to be sorry or to ask for forgiveness.

> **Truth**—*This rarely happens; in the meantime, I am in bondage!*

If I choose to forgive, I am acting like a hypocrite because I don't feel like forgiving.

> **Truth**—*I really am a hypocrite when I don't forgive, since I have Christ in me and He is a forgiving person. My feelings don't define me.*

I am afraid too many feelings will get stirred up.

> **Truth**—*God will guide you to gently get the feelings out that need to be healed.*[61]

Having removed the obstacles and objections to forgiveness, we are now ready to choose forgiveness. The person or persons need not be present or even living in order for you to release them. It would be good to quiet yourself before the Lord, separating from the anxiety and activity of everyday life. Focus on the cross, the payment that has already been made for all sin and wounds. Remind yourself that these offenses are *not* outstanding debts. They have all been paid in full at the cross. Let the weight of sin sit heavy within you as you are reminded of the terrible price that was necessary to relieve it.

Since the concept of forgiveness (and even the Greek word itself) is about release, it is absolutely necessary to hold the offense fully before you let it go. You cannot minimize the pain or the release will not be effective. In the parable of Jesus in Matthew 25, the king began by taking an account of his servants which revealed the weight of the debt.

Joanne was a leader in one of our ministries in the church. After her husband left her, she jumped into ministry with both feet. Everyone knew that if they assigned a ministry task to Joanne, it would be done. She was struggling, however, to get along with the other members of her team. She tended to work as a lone ranger rather than be a team player. As we sat to discuss this problem, I began to probe the effects of her divorce. I asked Joanne if she had forgiven her ex-husband. She nonchalantly answered, "Oh, sure, I forgave him right away. There is no sense in wallowing in it. He's gone and I'm better off for it." I was skeptical that real forgiveness had taken place, given the depth of emotion that is usually attached to divorce. I asked her how she felt about her husband leaving. She didn't answer as quickly this time. Finally she tried to speak, but instead began to cry. In the sessions that followed, we uncovered feelings of anger, fear, betrayal, inadequacy, and rejection that were causing Joanne to isolate from others to protect herself from further hurt. She hadn't really forgiven her husband because she had not adequately charged the debt that he had incurred. Once she connected the feelings and the lies to the offense, she was really ready to forgive.

The weight of the debt of sin involves the whole person. The sin was an act of the will and must be named. Speak or write the name of the person and the exact offense or offenses. The sin is also connected with your emotions. It made you feel a certain way. Try to put words to the emotions you felt when you sinned or were sinned against. Take some time here to allow the emotions to surface. If this sin or wound is the source of an unhealthy emotional pattern in you, you must feel the weight of it in order to experience the complete release. The sin also made an impact on your mind. Certain lies entered your mind as a direct result of this sin. Perhaps you labeled yourself a *loser* or *worthless*. Connect with the statements that seem to run through your mind when you think of this sin or wound. Talk this all out fully or journal it. Allow time for all these connections between the sin, your mind, will and emotions to be made. Now you are ready to approach the cross.

The cross is the place of forgiveness. Here the sins and wounds of the world were fully paid. You do not need to minimize this sin; it was severe enough to demand the death of the sinless Son of God. But it is paid for. The blood that was shed paid the price in full. You can release this sin to the cross where it is forgiven and removed, along with all of its associated lies and emotions. Give up these thoughts and emotions. Give up the right to judge the one who sinned. Give up the right to feel any differently. Give up the right to understand. Forgiveness is all about giving up and releasing.

You can release this sin to the cross where it is forgiven and removed, along with all of its associated lies and emotions.

It may help your focus during this process to have a cross or a picture of the cross in sight and have soft worship music playing in the background. Once all is released, open your hands before the Lord and receive the grace to walk away from this painful place in your life without the weight of this debt. Jesus paid it all.

I clearly recall working through this very forgiveness exercise early in my recovery process. I took a weekend to get away and focus on this life choice. With a wooden cross in front of me and soft worship music playing, I began to journal first about the acts of abuse against me. The list started slowly; but the more I wrote, the more seemed to flow out of me. Soon, the emotions began to surface. Anger, hurt, entrapment, confusion, controlled, overwhelmed, and weak—all of these were connected to these acts. Finally, I focused on what I believed about myself because of these acts and emotions. *I am weak. I am perverted. There is something wrong with me. I don't matter. I'm not like other boys.* Slowly the list grew.

When I felt that I had written all I could write, I allowed the emotions to surface, and I began to sob as I felt this pain and anger anew. As I sat in this place, the offense of the church rose up. The body of Christ had not offered me truth, refuge, or a safe place. For years I had sought the Father in church and had only hit the cold hard slab of law. I had to go back to the paper and charge this debt as well.

Finally, I began to release it all to the cross. Starting with the abuser, then those who did not protect me, then the church, I placed the sins on the cross where I knew they had been paid. Those who hurt me could never pay for these sins. I could not make these sins any better. But Jesus, the sinless Son of God was the "Lamb of God that takes away the sin of the world."[62]

There was such a relief as I let these go. These thoughts, feelings, and memories no longer have the power to haunt my journey. They no longer define me in any way. But I needed a marker, a visible display that I could return to as a reminder to combat the feelings when they resurfaced. I took a helium balloon and wrote the names of those who had sinned against me on it. I took the balloon outside and held it in my hand as I proclaimed my desire to fully release all of these wrongs to God. I let go of the balloon and watched it disappear into the presence of the One who paid for it all.

I am not going to tell you that the feelings never return. Different events or emotions can trigger a return to the memories of the abuse. I am not going to claim that I never have bad feelings toward those who hurt me (even the church). But when these feelings surface or these thoughts enter my head, I go back in my memory to the release of that balloon and remind myself that it is over. It has been released, and it has been forgiven.

If you are holding on to sin or wounds, forgiveness is God's way—the only way to healing and the only way to life. If this cloud remains between you and the Father, it will interfere with your ability to hear from Him, to worship Him, and to move toward intimacy with Him. Unforgiveness will also create an *edge* in you that will make true community and true surrender impossible. It is safe to let it all go; it is safe to move again into community because you know the One who can forgive all. It is time to let it all go. It is time to choose forgiveness, a choice that can be made because He has already paid for it all. Choose life!

Questions to Ponder—Chapter 7

1. In what ways does your experience attest to the teaching that unforgiveness ties you down and prevents you from walking in freedom?

2. Write in your own words why it is possible for followers of Jesus to forgive others.

3. Set aside some time to be alone with the Lord. Before you can receive God's forgiveness or extend it to someone who has wounded you, you must connect the sin/wound to the emotion that it produced.

"Father, I bring my heart and life before you now and invite you to reveal to me any areas of my life in which I have not received your forgiveness or any people in my life that I need to forgive. I have been bound by bitterness, hurt, guilt and shame, for far too long, and I want to be free. I also want to be free from the negative emotions that are associated with these sin and wounds. Guide me, Lord, as I make this step toward choosing forgiveness. In Jesus' name. Amen"

Now, make a list of the sin or wounds in the appropriate column on the chart. Include the name of the person that is the offender (self if it is your own sin). Now look at the list of possible emotions listed in Appendix 1 in the back of the book. When you think of this sin or wound, what emotion does it trigger? Write the emotions beside the offense in the appropriate column.

Sin or Wound List the offense and the offender	Emotion Use Appendix 1 to identify the feelings.

When you have finished filling in the chart. Take some time to sit with the Father. Perhaps have a cross to help you focus on the payment that has been made for all of these sin and wounds. One by one, offer each one to the Father and receive the full forgiveness that the cross paid for you.

4. Honestly record some of the reasons why you have been unable to forgive yourself and others for the sin and/or wounds listed above.

5. What truths have you learned in this lesson that address these obstacles to forgiving?

6. Write out your plan to appropriate and memorialize your choice to forgive.

CHAPTER 8

Choose Truth

❦

Renewing my mind with God's truth frees me from negative self-talk and affirms my true identity in Christ.

Football has never really been my sport. It takes coordination, speed, and physical power which aren't the highest on my list of abilities. But as a youth pastor for years, I have enjoyed my share of tackle football games played on sloping fields at camp. I never wanted to be the quarterback (too much pressure). I really didn't care much about being a receiver either. When you miss the ball it can be quite humiliating. I wanted to be the tackle. All I have to do is throw my body at the guy with the ball and make him fall to the ground. It doesn't take a lot of ability to do that. I did learn, early on in my career as an amateur tackle, that if you are going to throw your body at the guy with the ball, you want to aim for his feet. If you hit him high, he can regain his footing and run on. But, if you hit him low, knock out his footing, his foundation . . . he is toast and you are the man!

I am not really rambling here, but actually making a point. Striving and unforgiving with the corresponding guilt (because I can never strive hard enough) and shame (because I can never detach from my sin), form the foundation for the false self. When we choose grace and forgiveness, we are hitting the false self low and destroying its foundation. Choosing grace ends striving (guilt-free living) and choosing forgiveness releases me from shame. The chains have been released and we are free to begin taking off the lies, labels, masks, and trappings of this false persona that has become our identity and held us in bondage. We are ready to choose truth.

As we worked through forgiveness, we began to address some of the thoughts and feelings that were false and flowed from our sin and wounds. Now, we turn our attention to the totality of lies and deceptions that have helped to form our system for living up to this point. It is time to challenge these lies and choose truth.

We must begin by emphasizing the vital role of truth in our process of choosing life. Jesus told those who listened to Him that if they would hold to His teaching, they would be His disciples. As a result of being His disciples, they would know the truth, and the truth would set them free.[63] It is important to note that Jesus did not say that all who followed Him would be free. There is the requirement of holding to His teaching and really knowing the truth. Genuine freedom flows from the truth.

The Apostle Paul also emphasized the importance of truth. He instructed the Philippian believers to think or focus their attention on things that were true[64] and constantly spoke of the need to "renew our minds" with truth.[65] When He was addressing the embattled members of the church at Ephesus, he reminded them that their major battles were not against other people but against spiritual powers. They were instructed to "gird their loins" with truth,[66] which speaks to the need of being ready and able practically to apply the truth in all life situations.

With the multitude of thoughts and opinions available in our society, it is sometimes difficult to quantify the truth. What is truth? The good news for believers is that God has clearly identified His Word as the truth[67] and as the Words of life.[68] We have an absolute standard for truth that comes from the very mouth of God and carries the authority of the creator of the universe. What God says is true—period. It does not matter if life circumstances or feelings seem to contradict this truth. God's Word is true because it came from God and it cannot change.[69] Because of this, the truth of God's Word can form a solid foundation for building our true identity so that we can fully lay down the false self.

We have an absolute standard for truth that comes from the very mouth of God and carries the authority of the creator of the universe.

The problem is that our minds have not been clearly trained in the truth. As we grew up, before we knew the Lord, our spirit was dead within us and we were unable to hear the voice of God or recognize truth.[70] Instead of the presence of the Spirit of God transforming our minds from the inside, our minds were conformed to the thoughts, impressions, opinions, and world views of those who contributed to our upbringing. Consider three important sources of the system of belief that we have embraced apart from Christ.

First, voices from our past have spoken powerful messages to us. Our parents, peers, teachers, church leaders, and society in general have tried to put a label on us that is based upon how we are perceived in the world. Our behavior is quickly perceived as our identity and spoken aloud to us by important voices. We begin to believe that we are stupid, uncoordinated, ugly, fat, a problem child, worthless, a mistake, or weak. We can still hear the voice of someone in our past saying "You will never amount to anything;" or "How could you be so stupid?" Conversely, we may have heard words like, "You are so beautiful;" "You are so smart;" or "You are so athletic." While hearing these may not seem like a problem, if they become our identity, we are in bondage to maintaining the beauty, intelligence, or athleticism in order to be okay with who we are. Failure to maintain can be devastating. Without the power of the truth from within, we are left to believe these messages and form our identity around them.

Second, along with these voices, we add the interpretation of the circumstances of our lives. As children, we are excellent at recording these circumstances (we know what happened). We are immature and inadequate in our attempts to interpret them properly (we don't know what they mean). If our father was absent or passive, we may believe that we don't really matter because we don't seem to matter to him. If one of our parents leaves us, we may quickly assume we were at fault and have caused this pain. If we are abused, we may believe that we were at fault in some way and that there must be something wrong with us. If we fail in our attempts to accomplish certain tasks, we may begin to see ourselves as failures. If we are a little different from our peers and don't seem to fit in with them, we may assume that we don't belong and people will not include us. If the things we attempted never quite met the approval of those in authority over us, we may assume we don't measure up. These messages are not necessarily verbalized like the ones from the voices of our past. However, they are just as powerful because they are our own conclusions. Many times, with the voice from the past in our heads, it is easy to see the circumstances of our lives as confirmation of the voice's message.

Finally, the voice of the Enemy is added to the echo of lies in our thinking from the people and circumstances of our past. Scripture says that he is the father of all lies[71] and that deception is his number one tactic in his strategy to defeat us.[72] Playing on the information planted by the voices from our past and the misinterpretation of our circumstances, Satan builds a stronghold of lies to block us from the truth about who we really are and keep us captive by the lies.

This stronghold of lies forms the foundation for our negative self-talk and our negative identity. In his book, *Telling Yourself the Truth*,[73] William Backus explains that there are messages that play in our minds just under the radar of our conscious thought. These messages are like old MP3 files that continuously play in our subconscious thought and form the basis for our belief system. The person who will not try new things hears the voice of self-talk say, "Don't take a chance;" "You will only be hurt;" or "You are not the kind of person to try new things." The person who is afraid to let their emotions out hears the voice of self-talk say, "You can't handle this," "You will fall apart," or "It is not safe to share your feelings." The person who feels that they must always be right hears the voice of self-talk say, "You can't risk being wrong," or "You must be right in order to be accepted by others." This self-talk actually forms a system of rules for living that empowers our will to choose a certain course of action by default. We no longer even have to think about our response, because we have programmed ourselves by our beliefs (beliefs which just happen to be lies). This default setting of our will becomes a flesh pattern, habit, or even addiction that keeps us in bondage. It is a bondage that can only be broken by renewing our minds with the truth.

The voices of the past, misinterpretation of circumstances, and the Enemy cause us to believe lies that become the foundation for our lives.

Interestingly, it is this negative self-talk that provides us with the insight to move toward healing. It is often difficult to put words to the voices from our past or the way that we have interpreted our past. We can, however, with a little focus, pull our negative self-talk into our conscious thinking in order to identify the lies that we believe. We often wonder, *Why do I do the things that I do, why am I stuck in this pattern,* or *why do I always respond this same way?* If we will regularly journal our thoughts, especially in times of our greatest struggles, some of these negative statements of self-talk will rise to the surface and reveal a repeated pattern. As we write down these lies, we can then trace them back to people or circumstances where they may have taken root. This exercise is not attempted for the purpose of blaming someone from our past for our broken lives, but it often helps to identify the root cause of the misbeliefs and lies that trouble us.

The voices of the past, misinterpretation of circumstances, and the Enemy cause us to believe lies that become the foundation for our lives. These lies build up into a stronghold which controls the way we live. Out of this stronghold of lies, we develop certain rules by which we live and we develop default flesh patterns that become our own personal repeated ways of doing life (see Diagram 4). These flesh patterns actually determine our behavior because we have allowed them to become our default settings. Most of us think that our lives would improve if we could change

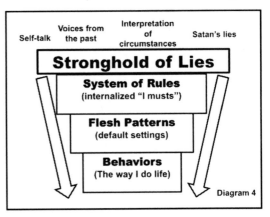

our behavior. However, our behavior is flowing out of flesh patterns that were put into place by a system of rules which were birthed out of lies we have believed from our past. We cannot effectively change behavior unless we destroy the stronghold that is driving it. We must replace the lies with truth.

Enrique came to me in a deep depression and addicted to prescription drugs. He attributed his downward spiral to the loss of his job and his inability to find a comparable position to support his family. While it was understandable that Enrique would be down about his circumstance, it seemed that his behavior was driven by a little more. As we explored the voices from his past, it became clear that Enrique believed that he should be able to fix everything, to make everything better. Failure was not an option in his family growing up; you did what you could and you made it better. Up to this point, this system of rules had worked for Enrique and even contributed to his previous success. The downward turn of the economy and the loss of his job put him in a situation that he could not fix. Because his entire identity had been built upon the lie that he should be able to fix anything, he felt like a complete failure and couldn't handle it. He needed to identify the lie about who he was and allow the Father to tell him his true identity, which did not require him to fix everything.

This process of identifying and dealing with the lies that fill our minds is a strategy that is recommended in Scripture as well. The Apostle Paul encouraged the church at Corinth to "take captive every thought to make it obedient to Christ" as a means of "demolish[ing] strongholds."[74] Also, as pointed out in the opening paragraphs of this chapter, the Apostle Paul provides guidance about renewing our minds. When we accept Christ as our Savior, we are given a new heart and are made a new creature. Our thinking, however, having been conformed to the unspiritual mindset of the world, must now be renewed—transformed from the inside—as the Spirit of God speaks truth to our hearts. Often it is said by Christians that they understand the truth with their minds but not with their hearts. Actually, it is just the opposite. The truth finds its place in the new heart of the believer; but the mind must be transformed by that new heart.

As we identify the negative self-talk that is common to our thinking, we can pinpoint the exact lies that drive the behavior of our false self. We can then renounce these as lies and replace the lie with the truth from God's Word. Choose truth! Finding Scripture to counteract the lies is a positive, healing activity that inspires us to move forward on our journey toward life. Scripture is truth. Scripture contains the words of life. Write out the truth, illustrate it with meaningful pictures, and post it in places where you can frequently be reminded of the discovered truth. This method was first proposed by God to the nation of Israel when they were ready to go into the Promised Land. He did not want them to forget His laws. So he challenged them to talk of them while walking, sitting, or standing and to write them on their foreheads and the doorposts of their home. This is a truth campaign, a strategy to renew our minds.

Where do we begin? I believe that it will be most beneficial to begin our healing at the same place that Satan normally begins his attack—our identity. When Jesus was tempted in the wilderness, Satan tried to use his physical weakness to challenge His identity. "If you are the Son of God, tell these stones to become bread."[75] He was attacking Jesus' identity, and this is the place he will most likely start with us. As you begin to delve into this area of lies about your identity, write in your journal some answers to the question, "Who am I?" Write down statements that you think define who you are. As you become comfortable that this list is an accurate reflection of what is really going on inside of you (choosing honesty again), you can begin to trace these statements backward to their source. Was there a voice from your past that spoke this to you? Did you decide this was who you were because of some circumstance or repeated pattern in your life?

Now begin to seek the truth about your identity, which is only available from the Father. As we learned earlier, your story began in the heart of the Father. Before the beginning of time, He picked up the pencil and wrote your name into His story. He created you. Though you were born a sinner, when you received Christ (chose grace), He gave you a new heart and a new identity. He alone knows who you really are, and He has shared His thoughts with you in His Word. One of the simplest places to find a clear declaration of your new identity in Christ is Ephesians chapter 1. The Apostle Paul had visited the city of Ephesus in Asia Minor (modern-day Turkey) on his missionary journeys. In fact, he spent more time there than in any other city he visited. He even helped to ordain the elders in that church. His fondness for these believers was evident in his words. As time progressed, Paul was made aware of some behavioral problems that had cropped up in the church. (Even the early church had problems.) He picked up his pen to address these behavioral problems. With this fact in mind, it is interesting that Paul never even mentioned their behaviors until the fourth chapter of the book. He spent the first three chapters reminding them of who they were (identity), and then he turned the conversation in chapter 4 and verse 1 to their *walk,* or behavior. Paul knew that understanding the truth about our true identity empowers us to live the life that is in us.

Ephesians 1 confirms several times that we, as believers, are "in Christ." If we picture this on our Life Chart, it is the position of life that we have chosen. When we stepped into life, it was not our life but Christ's life (see Diagram 5). He removed the sin and wounds by paying the full penalty for them all, and He took up residence in us and became the connection between us and the Father. He became our life. Since we now have Christ's life in us, it becomes the defining quality of who we are. Paul says that we have received "spiritual blessings" from the Father (verse 3). He then begins a list of these blessings, all of them pointing to our identity. In verse 4, Paul reminds us that we are chosen by God. Imagine this! You may have never been picked as the captain of the team, the supervisor of the office, the beauty queen, or the head deacon, but you have been picked by God. You are chosen, chosen to belong to Him, with His name

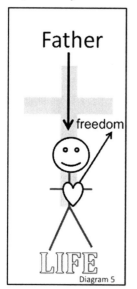

Diagram 5

written on your hand. In verse 5, Paul reminds them that they are adopted. Certainly they were born sinners, as were we all. But God did not leave us in that family; He chose to adopt us and make us His children. We are precious sons and daughters of the Father. The behavior problems that they were experiencing in the church did not change their identity. Behavior flows out of identity. They were still precious sons and daughters of God; they were just choosing not to act like it.

Ponder these two thoughts for a moment. You are chosen to be a precious son or daughter of the Father, the God of the universe, and the Creator of life. Imagine the value, the worth, and the prestige of such a position. Stand tall; hold your head up high. How can we begin to let the words of men and circumstances of life hold more power over our identity than the decrees of God?

Continuing in Ephesians 1 only serves to confirm and broaden this new identity. We are accepted by God (verse 6), redeemed and forgiven (verse 7), enlightened and full of wisdom (verses 8-9), and heirs of the eternal God (verses 10-11).

It is imperative at this point that we read, memorize, visualize, and meditate on these truths. The voices and circumstances of our past have been playing in our minds for far too long. They will not be silenced easily. A practical way to choose truth is to spend time in Ephesians 1 until we cannot only say with confidence who we really are in Christ but also believe it. Choose truth!

My own process through this life choice included another truth from Scripture. II Corinthians 5:21 says that Christ became sin for me so that I could become righteous. During my recovery process, those who supported and mentored me spoke this truth over me in prayer one day. I immediately recoiled. I am *not* righteous. My desires for sexual activity and deceit that flow from the false self are anything but righteous. In spite of my reaction, they continued to pray. Eventually, I began to sense that this label of righteous was *exactly* what the Lord wanted me to wear. He wanted me to see that He looked beyond me and my behaviors to the life of Christ that was in me. The life of Christ was righteous; so I was righteous. I began to say regularly, "I am a righteous man." At first it was difficult to say and even harder to believe. However, as I rehearsed it and claimed the truth of that verse of Scripture, I came to believe it. This new belief began to change the way I felt about myself *and* change the way that I behaved. I was tearing down the stronghold of lies with the truth of God's word. And the bonus is that since I am a righteous man, I can choose to live righteously. Choosing truth IS choosing life.

You are chosen to be a precious son or daughter of the Father, the God of the universe, and the Creator of life.

Questions to Ponder—Chapter 8

1. Explain in your own words how the wounds of your past affect your ability to walk in truth today.

2. Take some time to identify several wounds from your past that still produce pain when you think about them. Use the chart below to record a false belief that grew out of that wound. Finally, record a truth from God's Word that exposes and corrects the lie-based thought.

Past Wound	A Lie I Believed	God's Truth
e.g. My father left us when I was small.	e.g. People are unreliable. Trust no one!	e.g. "I will never leave you nor forsake you". God will never abandon me!

3. The Enemy most often speaks to us in first-person pronouns (I, me, my). Describe the process of discerning lies and truth.

4. How does "negative self-talk" contribute to your particular struggle?

5. Read Ephesians 1 and make a list of everything it says about you as a believer in Christ.

6. Use Appendix 2 to learn your true identity in Christ. Which of these new labels would help you to combat the negative labels you have been wearing? Write them down below, memorize, visualize, and meditate on them.

CHAPTER 9

Choose Surrender

ℭℌ

*Laying down my shame, coping mechanisms and masks frees me
to find life completely in the Father.*

In the Disney film *Finding Nemo*, Marlin is a clown fish looking for his young son Nemo. He finds himself, along with his memory-impaired friend Dory, in the mouth of a whale. They are lying on the whale's tongue when all of a sudden things begin to shift. The tongue moves up, the water begins to rush toward the back of the throat, and Marlin panics. He believes that the whale is trying to swallow them, so he clings tightly to the tongue, urging Dory to do the same. Finally, Dory decides to let go of the tongue and flow with the water. She tells Marlin to do the same. Marlin asks the question, "How do you know something bad isn't going to happen?" Dory answers with truth, "You don't!" They both let go and end up being blown out of the whale through the water spout instead of being swallowed. Sometimes, in order to move toward healing, you just have to let go. Surrender!

So far on this journey toward life, we have dealt with most of the obstacles to life pictured on the right-hand side of the Life Chart. We have chosen grace and forgiveness to remove our sin and wounds. We have chosen truth to remove the lies and labels that have formed the basis for the false self. We are now ready to deal with the false self through surrender. It is time to lay down our shame, surrender our coping mechanisms, and set aside our masks.

At some point in His earthly ministry, Jesus set His face toward the cross. The time for Him to lay down His life had come, and He needed to surrender to the Father's plan. Scripture tells us that Jesus went into a small garden called

Gethsemane on the side of the hill known as the Mount of Olives. Small olive trees and other plants grew in a serene setting. It was evening. Jesus separated from His disciples and went alone to pour out His heart to the Father in prayer. The physical pain and spiritual anguish that lay ahead was weighing heavily. He needed this time with the Father. As He rose to leave from this difficult time of prayer, He finally spoke the words of surrender, "Not my will, but Yours be done."[76] Jesus surrendered. He laid down His own desires and comfort to be a part of the larger plan.

Jesus came to give us life, to offer life as an every-moment possibility for all of us. He declared this as His purpose on more than one occasion.[77] He also taught that unless we surrender our lives, we can't really follow Him into life; we can't be His disciple.[78］ *Surrender isn't suggested as a way to the life we were always meant to live; it is required.* Surrender isn't suggested as a way to the life we were always meant to live; it is required. It is not, however, a tool to be used to manipulate God into giving us what we want, nor is it a way to gain favor with God. Surrender is a spiritual discipline. The simplest definition of a spiritual discipline is that it is a practice that works to make space in our lives for God, a space to recognize His presence and power, a space to experience who He is and His plan for life.

> "The purpose of the Disciplines is freedom. Our aim is the freedom, not the Discipline. The moment we make the Discipline our central focus, we turn it into law and lose the corresponding freedom. The Disciplines have value only as a means of setting us before God so that He can give us the liberation we seek . . . they (the Disciplines) are NOT the answer. We must clearly avoid this limitation of the Disciplines if we are to avoid bondage."[79]

When we surrender, we let go of the clutter in our lives and make room to experience God and His desires and that experience is life—the life we were created to live.

In the same passage where Jesus taught us that surrender is required, He also defined surrender. He basically taught us that surrender has two sides: self-denial (take up your cross) and trust (follow me).[80] In *Finding Nemo*, Marlin had to let go of his fears and desire for safety and follow Dory. Jesus had to let go of His own desire not to suffer and trust God's plan. We must do the same.

These two aspects of surrender are illustrated well in the extreme sport of bungee jumping. The daredevil climbs to a high place, fastens one end of the bungee cord to his ankle, the other end to a solid foundation. The thrill of bungee jumping can never be experienced, though, unless there is surrender. Standing on the cliff, bridge, or elevated platform with the cord firmly attached does *not* qualify as bungee jumping. To experience the thrill of the free fall, he actually has to JUMP! He has to surrender, deny himself the safety of the foundation he is standing on, and trust the strength of the cord that is tied around his ankle (Christ) to keep him firmly connected to the foundation (Father). When he surrenders, he experiences the thrill, the exhilaration, and the sheer TERROR of bungee jumping. Maybe we have never pictured ourselves as someone who would take such a risk but, hang on, here we go!

Surrender begins with self-denial. We must do a self-assessment to determine the role of our shame, our coping mechanisms, and our masks. We can't lay them down until we know what they are. Let's use some of the following questions to help in this assessment.

1. Do I feel less valued than others?
2. Do I worry that if people really knew me, they wouldn't like me?
3. Do I accept my physical appearance?
4. Do I avoid calling any attention to myself, even if I am doing positive things?
5. Do I tend to put myself down and criticize myself?
6. Do I believe that I must always be happy?
7. Do I believe that I must always feel good?
8. Do I believe that I must be able to fix problems?
9. Do I believe that I must be in control?
10. Do I believe that I must always get my way?
11. Do I believe that I must be free of all sin struggles in order to be acceptable to God?
12. How does my public persona differ from my inner self?
13. How do I usually feel after spending time in public?
14. Do I avoid things that I am not good at?

15. When I am in pain, do I turn to something other than God for relief?
16. How freely do I share my emotions?

It is important that we spend some time here. As we look at the answers to the questions above, we should be able to begin a list of things that we need to surrender. The answers to questions 1-5 will reveal if we are living under a cloak of shame. What is causing this shame; why do we feel less valued than others? In the classic movie *Les Miserables,* Jean Valjean has spent 19 years in prison for stealing food to feed his family. He is released but cannot find a place to rest or get a meal. Finally he knocks on the door of a bishop. As he stands in the doorway, he keeps a heavy cloak over his head and identifies himself as a very dangerous convict. He has taken his identity from his past behavior, and he is ashamed of who he is. Part of the beauty of this film is in the scene where the bishop throws back the cloak and pronounces a new identity over this former convict. If the answers to these first questions reveal any shame about who you are, it must be surrendered. Jesus died on the cross for our sin but also for our shame. He was shamed in many ways so that we could stand in the presence of the Father with our heads held high—proud of who we are in Christ.

The answers to questions 6-11 will reveal something about our coping mechanism and how we deal with the fact that in this fallen world, life doesn't always turn out the way we want. If we cope by always trying to be happy, feel good, in control, get our way, or free ourselves from struggle, we are trying to make our lives work on our own terms. We are not finding our life completely in our relationship with the Father. These ways of coping with life must be surrendered. We don't have to be happy, pain free, free of struggles, in control, or have our way in order to experience life.

Finally, the answers to questions 12-16 will help to reveal what mask we usually wear when interacting with other people. Are we free to be ourselves, or do we have to perform in a certain way in order to be okay? Do we try to be acceptable by being smart, funny, efficient, loving, creative, athletic, generous, or musical? These qualities are great if they flow out of our heart and are not what we use to determine our identity. If we depend on these things to be okay with ourselves, they need to be surrendered. We must get our identity totally from Christ and then allow these things to flow out of that identity.

I shared in a previous chapter that I viewed my identity as coming from my role as the perfect pastor (my own illusion). I made attempts to find healing while still serving in that role but found that I needed to completely surrender that persona—that mask—and learn to live out of my true identity in Christ from my good heart. I am again serving in the role of a pastor, but now it is not *who I am;* it is just what I do.

Surrender involves coming to the realization that we are not the center of the universe. Life doesn't have to be done the way we think it should be done. We come to the realization that what we want (our desire) does not have to be the driving factor of our lives (permission to act).

This kind of self-denial is radical. It cuts against our flesh and experience. It leads to death—the death of self. This is why Jesus used the phrase "take up your cross" when referring to surrender. If, in the Roman culture of the day, someone was carrying a cross out of the village, it was certain that he wasn't coming back. The cross meant death. We must die to self in order to really experience the life that God has for us because the false self is grounded in self—not in God.

Surrender involves coming to the realization that we are not the center of the universe.

Let's identify with Peter, Jesus' disciple, as we walk through this life choice. Peter was called by Jesus to "follow me." Peter left his nets, his family, his business and his livelihood to follow Jesus.[81] This is surrender. As we follow the life of Peter from that point, though, we begin to see areas of his life that were not surrendered. He often struggled to understand what Jesus meant by his teachings. He regularly said things just to make himself look good, revealing a need that had not been surrendered. When he was faced with the possibility of imprisonment or death after the arrest of Jesus, he cracked under the pressure of questions from a young girl and cursed the name of Jesus. Peter had not surrendered his life fully to Jesus.

We may feel that we have surrendered to the Lord but, like Peter, God uses events and life circumstances to reveal areas of our lives that are not surrendered. The way that we parent our children may reveal our need to control their lives in an effort to look good as parents. The way we take care of our physical bodies may reveal our need to look good in order to be okay or conversely, our desire to be invisible in a crowd. Our inability to sit in discomfort or pain without relying on our coping mechanisms may reveal a dependence on feeling good. Self-denial may mean that we don't always look good to others and that we don't always feel good.

As we move toward this goal of self-denial and surrender, it is important not to push too far. Self-denial is *not* self-hatred. We don't lose our identity by denying who we are. We embrace our new identity in Christ and live our new role as child of God, while at the same time, denying our flesh the control over this new self. Self-denial is also not self-contempt where we blame ourselves for every wrong that happens and constantly criticize ourselves, fueled by feelings of worthlessness. In Christ, we have tremendous value and are the object of His unconditional love. Self-denial is also not self-pity, wallowing in what we have given up for the Lord or what we have failed to do. The Apostle Paul said that the things that he gave up for Christ, he counted as dung[82] (there are other words to use here, but you get the point) compared to the new life he had in Christ.

As we journey forward toward wholeness, there are some tell-tale signs or indications that we may not have surrendered some things. One of these signs is weariness. Being the center of the universe is exhausting, and if we haven't let go of control, we will be tired. If negative feelings or negative circumstances always cause our coping mechanisms to kick into gear instead of triggering dependence on God, we still need to surrender. If being in a crowd of people that we feel *have it all together* causes us to put on an act or withdraw in timidity, we still have need to surrender. If we are still striving with these things, we are not enjoying the rest that Jesus came to give. Surrender.

Another sign that we have not surrendered is constant questioning of God. Our *need to know* the reasons that things are happening or our drive to *make sense of it all* will siphon off our faith and leave us bitter and doubting. We haven't surrendered the *need to know*.

This brings us to the second part of surrender—trust. If we go back to the bungee jumping illustration, once we have denied ourselves the safety of the platform, it is time to fully trust the cord. Scripture teaches us that trust is both leaning into God and acknowledging Him in all circumstances.[83] Trust is *knowing* that God wants us to grow and experience life and that He loves us and cares about our journey. If we don't really know who God is, it will be difficult to surrender to Him. Scripture reveals God as:

Creator of the universe (Genesis 1)
The Almighty One (Genesis 17:1, 2)
The Lord who Provides (Genesis 22:14)
The Lord who Heals (Exodus 15:22-26)
The Lord our Peace (Judges 6:24)
The Lord our Shepherd (Psalm 23:1)
The Lord our Shield (Psalm 3:3)
The Lord our Deliverer (Psalm 18:2)
The Lord our Strength (Psalm 22:19)
The Lover of our Soul (Jeremiah 31:3)
The God who Cares (Matthew 6:25-34)
Our Father (Matthew 6:9)

This is the kind of God we can trust. We may want to spend some time looking at these verses and getting to know God better so that we can surrender our trust completely to Him.

Trust almost presupposes the absence of feeling. If we always feel God's love and presence, there is no real need for trust. Trusting is continuing to believe it, even when we can't feel it. In his book, *Ruthless Trust*, Brennan Manning puts it this way,

> "The reality of trust is the life of a pilgrim who leaves what is nailed down, obvious and secure and walks into the unknown without any rational explanation to justify the decision or guarantee the future. Why? Because God has signaled the movement . . .."[84]

The struggle with addiction is often fueled by a desire that won't go away. Even after the Lord convinces us that this addiction must be denied, the strong desire to continue in it remains. Trusting God means denying ourselves the pleasure of the addiction—in spite of the strong desire to give in to it—believing that following God will ultimately bring greater satisfaction than the fulfillment of this fleshly desire. Surrender is not dependent on the removal of the desire. In fact, the desire is the very thing that must be surrendered and denied, leaning into the power of God to do so. It is actually the continued presence of this desire that triggers our trust in God.

I have worked extensively with men who struggle with same-sex attraction. Many of them had experiences early in life that bent them toward men in a sexual way. This "bent" was not their choice. But living as a homosexual is a choice. As many of these men work through their issues and move toward healing, the greatest desire is that their attractions may change. A frequently asked question is "When am I going to be attracted to women?" Choosing life is not dependent on this attraction changing. Choosing life is surrendering to follow Christ in obedience in spite of the desire that may or may not ever go away. Many men who do not struggle with same-sex attraction wish that their desire for other women would go away after they marry; but this is rarely the case. They must surrender to follow Christ in obedience in spite of their desire. The same may be true of your desire to overeat, to drink excessively, to gamble, or to spend too much time on the computer.

Trust does not mean inactivity; it simply means that as we act, we act in dependence on Him.

In the Old Testament, we meet a man named Job. He lost his wealth, his children and his health. In his despair, his wife advised him to "curse God and die."[85] Put yourself in Job's place. I am sure that He felt like cursing God and dying, but his feeling was not the point. His feeling was to be surrendered to the greater plan of God. His response reveals that he had chosen surrender. "Shall we accept good from God and not trouble?"[86] Job was trusting God in spite of his own feelings and circumstances.

In the New Testament, the Apostle Paul admitted while he lay in a prison cell that he had a desire to die and go to be with the Lord.[87] But he immediately recognized the greater good of staying to minister to these new believers at Philippi, so he surrendered that desire, trusting God that His plan was the best.[88]

Again, it is important that we don't move past trust into passivity or fatalism. Trust does not mean inactivity; it simply means that as we act, we act in dependence on Him. Trusting does not mean that we are waiting on the Lord to remove our desire or change our circumstances. Trusting means that we lean into Him for strength in spite of our circumstances. Our trust is in Him, not in what we think He should do.

Trust doesn't mean clarity. We are not trusting in a clear picture that the Lord reveals to us about how to move forward. We are trusting in Him to guide us, one step at a time. Brennan Manning drives this point home with the following illustration:

> "When the brilliant ethicist John Kavanaugh went to work for three months at 'the house of the dying' in Calcutta, he was seeking a clear answer as to how best to spend the rest of his life. On the first morning there he met Mother Teresa. She asked, 'And what can I do for you?' Kavanaugh asked her to pray for him. 'What do you want me to pray for?' she asked. He voiced the request that he had borne thousands of miles from the United States: 'Pray that I have clarity.' She said firmly, 'No, I will not do that.' When he asked her why, she said, 'Clarity is the last thing you are clinging to and must let go of.' When Kavanaugh commented that she always seemed to have the clarity he longed for, she laughed and said, 'I have never had clarity; what I have always had is trust. So I will pray that you trust God.'"[89]

There are, of course, signs that we are not trusting God. When we are overcome with worry and anxiety, it is an indication that we have not surrendered the need to make things happen, that we are trusting in ourselves and not God. When we are wallowing in shame, guilt, and self-hatred because of our past, it is revealing a lack of genuine trust in the love, forgiveness, and redemption that was purchased for us by the blood of Christ. When we continue to wander, looking for life in places other than our relationship with God, it is revealing that we don't really believe that He and He alone is the source of life.

Surrender is denying self and trusting the Father. Surrender is the path to genuine encounters and experiences with the Father we cannot have when we hold on to self. When Jesus entered the Garden of Gethsemane, knowing what lay ahead, surrender was required to allow the experience of the cross. Jesus' comfort was not the point; the greater good for the Kingdom of God was accomplished because Jesus was willing to fully surrender to do the Father's will. The result of His surrender was life.

We've been standing on the platform far too long. It's time to jump; it's time to surrender!

Chapter 9—Questions to Ponder

1. Which illustration of surrender in this chapter did you connect with the most? Why?

2. Which of the following parts of "self" do you need to deny (say no to)?

_____ I need to be in control
_____ I need to make things happen
_____ I need to fix it
_____ I need to feel good
_____ I need to be happy
_____ I need to get my way
_____ I need to understand all that is going on in my life
_____ I need to look good to others
_____ I need to correct others' wrongs
_____ I need to share my opinion (speak my mind)
_____ I need to give in to the desire to _____
_____ Other: _____

3. Have you misinterpreted self-denial and fallen into self-hatred, self-contempt, or self-pity? Explain.

4. Does your life bear witness to a lack of self-denial (weariness or questionings)? Explain.

5. Some people trust in God and others trust in what they believe God should do. What do you trust in? What name for God (see the list in this chapter) do you most relate to?

6. Do you believe God is trustworthy? Why or why not? How will your answer to this question affect your ability to surrender?

7. Write out your goal for this healing process in a simple statement.

8. Does this statement reveal that you have surrendered all to the Father?

Choose Empowerment

Submitting to the power of the Spirit in me aligns my will with the will of the Father and frees me from the tyranny of the flesh.

What do you think of when you hear the word *power*? Is it a huge piece of construction equipment able to lift heavy objects; a powerful rocket engine exploding with power to push a huge payload into space; or a position of decision-making and leadership over large groups of people? Whatever image comes to mind when you hear the word power, you are either drawn to it with desire or you shrink from it with fear. Both of these responses reveal brokenness in the positive identity the Father gave mankind at creation (see Chapter 3).

We were created with power. After God created man and gave him the gift of life, he immediately gave him the gift of power; the ability to choose, to determine his own destiny. God prepared the Garden of Eden for man and gave him freedom in the Garden. Since God created man with the power of choice, He also had to give man an opportunity to use that power. God said that man could eat of any tree in the Garden, but the tree of knowledge of good and evil was off limits. The day Adam and Eve chose to eat of that tree, they would experience death instead of life. Everyday Adam and Eve chose life, until the fateful day that Eve was deceived by the Serpent and Adam passively chose to go along with Eve by eating the forbidden fruit. They had been using their power to choose life, but they had now used their power to choose death. The death they chose was separation from the Father, the source of life and the source of their real power. Compounding this separation was their new knowledge of good and evil which gave them a false confidence in their ability to experience real life independent of God. They knew what it felt like to gratify the flesh, and because of their separation from the Father, this new desire began to eclipse their desire for God. They lost their power to choose Him. Mankind began to do a sort of dance with power. Cain, the first son of Adam and Eve, used his power and chose to ignore God's way. He chose instead to pursue his own way, a way which ultimately led to the first murder. Mankind used fallen power to choose to build a tower to God at Babel, and they were rejected for their effort. Abraham chose to use his power of choice to follow God's direction in leaving his family and hometown in order to establish a new nation. Abraham was rewarded with blessing. Now, depending on our own history with power or the way power was used against us in our sin and wounds, we either desire to become more powerful or we embrace our weakness and submit to the power of others in unhealthy ways. This is the birth of the narcissist or the co-dependent—a dimension of the false self that will only experience healing when we understand the truth about power.

While some people are clearly narcissists and others clearly co-dependent, most people could be described as leaning toward one or the other. It may be helpful as we try to connect with our own belief about power for us to mark the continuum in Diagram 6 as we discuss these two dimensions of the false self.

Co-dependent   **Narcissist**

Diagram 6

The narcissist decides that he must use the power in him to control others. This power becomes the center of who he is, and he controls others with this self-focus. He uses anger, guilt, shame, or sheer force to manipulate others in his community to allow their lives to revolve around him. He has a sense of power, but it is a power that comes from self and feeds on the powerlessness of others. The narcissist is not free to love others; he can only love others if they promote him and bow to his power. Anyone who does not submit to his power is considered disloyal and is cut off from relationship.

A teenager named John was brought to me by his parents because of his constant acting out in rebellious ways. John sat slouched in the chair across from me, head down, coat pulled up around his face, trying his best not to care about the fact that he had been dragged into the pastor's office against his will. Most of my initial questions were met with a shrug or a "whatever" response. John was presenting himself both at home and in my office as a young person who didn't care what others thought of him. He wanted to be seen as an individual who "did his own thing." The truth was that John cared very much what others thought. He had a strong desire to be the center of attention and control his world. He had chosen the route of rebellious acts, which would engage his parents and others in negative attention. When the negative attention came, he would adopt the "I don't care" attitude which caused those in his life to pursue him all the more. That was just what he wanted. John was a narcissist. He had found a way to use his power, through rebellious acts, to help control his family and the people around him.

Relational idolatry is trying to find life in another person other than God.

The co-dependent tends to feel powerless and thus decides to connect himself to another who seems to have power. He "comes alive" when he is able to "prop up" someone else by serving, praising, or being used by him. He experiences power through another, usually a narcissist. He not only plays into the building up of the narcissist's self-focus, but also loses his own identity in the process. It is hard for him (the co-dependent) to see himself apart from others, to separate his feelings from the feelings of others, or even have an opinion at all. He is so enmeshed in others' lives that he cannot separate completely from them. Another, and possibly more accurate, name for co-dependency is relational idolatry. It truly is trying to find life in another person other than God.

This is not how the Father created us. He created us with a power that flowed from our connection of life with Him. The living spirit within us was able to draw power from our connection with the Father, make good choices, and use that power to glorify Him. Every time Adam and Eve chose to eat of the tree of life, driven by the God-given desire for life in them, they brought glory to the Father. With their sin and the resultant disconnection from the Father, their spirit became dead just as God had predicted when He said ". . . you shall surely die." This dead spirit could no longer influence their will to choose God. The only influences left on their wills were their mind and emotions, fueled by their new-found knowledge of good and evil. This condition has been passed down to us. We act because we believe something to be true or right (mind), or we act because we feel something deeply (emotion), even if that feeling is self-serving. Both of these motivations are very subjective and fall prey to the fallen desires of man. The sinful nature passed on to us from Adam (and schooled by the stronghold of lies from our own journey) rules our mind and emotions, thus controlling the power of choice exercised by our will (see Diagram 7).

So using Diagram 7, we can see that the narcissist has learned through his journey that he is the center of the universe. He feels good when others praise and serve him. The selfishness of his sinful nature uses these beliefs (mind) and feelings (emotions) to convince the will to make choices that will promote self. The co-dependent believes that he has no power and must get his sense of being from another. He believes (mind) that he is powerless, worthless, and useless unless connected to someone with power in a co-dependent relationship. He also feels bad (emotions) about himself unless he is contributing to that other. So he abdicates his power and gives it to the other. Both are stuck because their will is being empowered by their minds and emotions which are controlled by their sinful natures.

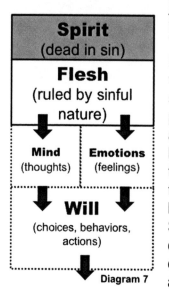

Diagram 7

This sounds hopeless, as if we are destined for failure. That is exactly how the Apostle Paul felt after describing his own will battle in Romans 7. He exclaims, "What a wretched man I am. Who will rescue me from this body of death?"[90] It is the right question because in order to escape the tyranny of the sinful nature—our flesh and the wrong choices of our will—we must be rescued by another. Andy Comiskey, in his text for *Living Waters*, concludes: "In order to walk out of life-dominating sin, we need His greater power to break into our lives. We need a will greater than our own."[91]

When we choose life by choosing Christ as our life, we do indeed receive a will greater than our own. We have chosen to reconnect with the Father through the life of Christ who died and rose again for us. In our journey toward life, we have already chosen to be honest about our fallen power and the ways we have used it to try to find life. We have also chosen to surrender our fallen power and all of our striving by choosing grace and the path toward healing, not self-effort. We have chosen to receive and extend forgiveness toward those who have tainted our view of power. With the release of these sins and wounds, we release the lies that are attached to them. In their place we have chosen truth. As we begin to embrace the truth, our minds are being renewed, and we come to the place of surrendering all of the wrong motives and desires that have empowered our will up to this point on our journey. Now we are ready to choose empowerment, to choose to allow the power of Christ to rise up in us, flow through us, and empower our will to choose. Choose life.

> *When we choose life by choosing Christ as our life, we do indeed receive a will greater than our own.*

The Apostle Paul taught the Christians in the region of Galatia in Asia Minor that when Christ was crucified, they died with Him. Christ bore their sinful nature to the cross and it died there. It no longer has the exclusive power to influence our will. It is dead. How much power does a dead man have? With the death of Christ and our sinful nature, there is also a resurrection. Christ—the resurrected Christ—lives in us![92] We have a new connection to the Father through His son Jesus. This new connection now makes it possible for our living spirit to influence once again our will just like it did for Adam and Eve before sin. Every day, just as they chose the tree of life, we can choose life. Now instead of allowing our mind and emotions ruled by our old sinful nature to empower our will, we can allow our spirit, which is connected to the Father, to empower our will. Not only that, but our mind is also being renewed by the truth from the Father. It actually begins to collaborate with our spirit in empowering our will to choose life. This is why the Apostle Paul told the church in Philippi that they could do all things through the power of Christ in them.[93]

Imagine you have a huge train set with multiple tracks and various places within the layout where you can switch tracks to alter the route of the train. These "switches" are battery-powered and have a button to push to change the train to another track. Let's imagine that as the train approaches one of these switches, you desire to change the route of the train, so you press the button, but nothing happens. The train continues down the same path it has been traveling; it does not change tracks. As you examine the problem, you find that the battery in the switch is dead because it has no power. It doesn't take a rocket scientist to know how to fix the problem. Replace the dead battery with a live one. Even after replacing the battery, you still have to press the button in order to change the direction of the train. In the same way, our switch (will) has a dead battery (sinful nature) and does not have the power to change the direction of our lives. We need a new battery (the living Spirit of God) with the power to change the direction of our lives. Even with the new battery, we still have to use our power of choice to push the button (choose). The good news is that we have all we need to do just that.

It sounds so easy. If our sinful nature which powered this whole thing is dead, why are we still stuck in recovery? Why is it that we seem to be unable to use this power of the living spirit of Christ in us to defeat the destructive thoughts and behaviors with which we struggle? Flesh. The sinful nature is dead, defeated, impotent, but our flesh patterns remain. The patterns that we developed in our lives while we were relying on the mind and emotion driven by our sinful nature to empower our will are deeply embedded in our reactions and our tendencies. They are directly opposed to the work of the Spirit in us and do not lead us to life but lead us to death.[94] How do we oppose these strong desires and choose life? It is important here that we see how Diagram 7 has changed since we chose Christ. The sinful nature no longer controls us. But the flesh patterns (less powerful) remain and can influence our mind, emotion and will. However, we are now completely immersed in Christ. His Spirit and His power will trump the flesh every time (see Diagram 8). We are more than conquerors through Christ.[95]

Our will, however, has atrophied over time as we have given in to the flesh. Galatians chapter 5 is clear that we must choose between the spirit and the flesh. The good news is that because of God's Spirit within us, we can choose life at any moment (have we said that?). We can align our desires and our wills with His. This does not mean that our fleshly desires will go away. It *does* mean that our desire to do the will of our Father rises above the desires of the flesh. This is exactly what happened to Christ before the cross. The desire of His flesh was that the suffering be avoided. He named that desire, but then exercised His will to yield that desire to the Father and align His will with the Father's. Have we aligned our will with the Father's? Are we in recovery because we want to feel better, want people to like us, to appear more spiritual and together, or because someone forced us to deal with our issues? We must stand before the

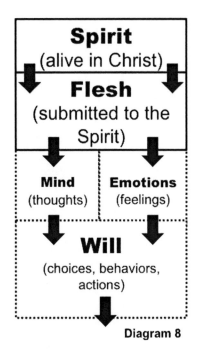

Diagram 8

cross naked and face our truest desires. For some, our desires are still primarily driven by our flesh. We still really just want to feel better, to stop a certain behavior, or to be more acceptable to God and others. If this is our desire, then our will is not aligned with His and there is no power. Aligning our will with God's comes when what we really desire is His will, not our comfort, not our pleasure, and not our way. Choosing empowerment is choosing to submit our will to the Father in every area of our lives. When Jesus went to the cross, he gave up (surrendered) all of his rights to comfort, his own way, and his own desires. He completely aligned his will with the Father's, no matter what that meant for him. Alexander Schmemann puts it this way ". . . to know that there is only one sin: not wanting God and being separated from Him; and there is only one sorrow, not having . . . unity with the One who is holy."[96]

While aligning our desires with His, we must also be aware of the tendency of our flesh toward passivity. As long as we remain passive, not tapping in to the power of Christ, we are the victim and we will remain stuck. (We have the new battery but refuse to press the button.) After we reconnect to the Father through Christ, passivity is a choice we make because aggressive realigning of our will is now possible. (We can change the course of this train.) In *The Healing Presence*, Leanne Payne writes,

> "Sometimes we discover that we just plain want to hang on to the sinful behavior, and some of us even have to face the fact that we then hope to blame God for not healing us. We see right away when we are dealing with a passive will, someone who looks lumpishly to a counselor or minister or to God to do what only he himself can do. All such things as these come to the fore, along with the memories of where the heart opened itself to envy, bitterness, lust and so on. Then, in full confession of our sins to God, we acknowledge our rank foolishness and our basic propensities to pride and rebellion, and we make a decision about sin."[97]

Choosing empowerment is not a one-time choice. It is a lifetime of yielding to the Spirit in us and a realignment of our wills. As I have moved forward on my own journey of healing, I have been at times plagued by my flesh. One of the ways that my flesh influences me is with the lure toward pornography. Sometimes the desire feels overwhelming and I have given in. Why did I do this? The answer is simple, because I wanted to. I wanted to feel good more than I wanted to do the Father's will. My fleshly desires were empowering my will and my will was not aligned with His. I was not in alignment and therefore had no power. I would not be clicking on these internet sites unless I wanted to. I am certainly not going against my own will. The fact is that I have set my own will and the desires of my flesh *against* the Father's will. I must align my desires with His desire for purity and deny my own desire to gratify my flesh (feel good in the moment). When my fleshly desires rise to the top (which they will), I must repent and realign my will with His much stronger will. The victory is found in that alliance. Choose empowerment!

Chapter 10—Questions to Ponder

1. What is my attitude toward power? How has my history of sin and wounds helped to form that attitude?

2. Read Galatians 2:20 and write in your own words how receiving Christ changes your "powerlessness."

3. Do you lean more toward behaving like a narcissist or co-dependent? Explain.

4. If you stood naked before the cross and faced the true desires of your heart, what would they be? Is there some realignment that still needs to take place?

5. How has passivity kept you stuck in your healing process?

6. Write out a prayer of repentance for all of your desires that are not aligned with God's will. Be sure to include any tendency toward passivity. Begin to pray this prayer at times of vulnerability and struggle, aligning your will with His at the moment of crisis.

CHAPTER 11

Choose Community

⚡

Developing healthy relationships frees me from unhealthy attachments and co-dependency.

Plastic is a wonderful invention. It is durable, versatile, recyclable, and cheap. However, some things should *not* be made of plastic. In our kitchen we have nice, heavy wood cabinets. Several drawers are built into the cabinets to house our silverware, dish towels, and kitchen sundries. One day, I noticed that one of the drawers had fallen and was not fitting correctly into the cabinet. I couldn't easily slide the drawer out and retrieve the fork, dish rag, or the "thingy" that I needed to open the pickle jar. Upon investigation, I found that the little slide that keeps the drawer in place was broken. The little slide is made of plastic, plastic which breaks when too much pressure is put upon it. The little plastic slide had to hold the weight of the drawer, plus all of its contents. Evidently, someone had put more into the drawer than the little plastic slide could handle and it had broken. The little plastic slide keeps the relationship between the cabinet and the drawer in correct alignment and smooth working order. Although the drawer can be taken in and out, tried and retried, unless the little plastic piece is repaired, the relationship between the cabinet and the drawer will remain less than ideal and not function properly. *Brokenness affects relationships.*

Our lives may appear strong and beautiful on the outside, like my kitchen cabinets. But if a small piece of us is broken, our relationships will be less than ideal. We will not enjoy community the way God intended, and we will not seem to fit well with others. As we have moved through the life choices in this book, we have become aware that we all have broken parts—the parts of our life that are broken and are not strong or healthy enough to support solid relationships. These broken parts not only hurt us; they greatly affect our ability to enter into authentic and meaningful relationships with others. For example, the sin and wounds in our lives have shattered our trust in others and broken the sense of belonging intrinsic to the positive identity that God created in us (see Diagram 1). Many times it is these difficult relationships with others that drive us to seek counsel or healing. Hopefully, we have learned that the broken relationships do *not* define our problem, but are a symptom of the deeper problems we have dealt with in earlier chapters.

Having dealt with some of these root problems, we are now ready to move into healthy relationships, to move into community, to choose community. If we were able to find a model where true community worked perfectly, it would help us discern what we may be missing. As with everything else in our lives, the perfect model is found in God. In the book, *The Sacred Romance,* the authors describe how it all began:

> "The story that is the sacred romance begins not with God alone, the Author at his desk, but God in relationship, intimacy beyond our wildest imagination, heroic intimacy. The Trinity is at the center of the universe; perfect relationship is the heart of all reality. Think of your best moments of love or friendship or creative partnership, the best time with family or friends around the dinner table, your richest conversations, the acts of simple kindness that sometimes seem like the only things that make life worth living. Like the shimmer of sunlight on a lake, these are reflections of the love that flows among the Trinity. We long for intimacy because we are made in the image of perfect intimacy."[98]

So God, the God that lived in intimate relationship from the beginning of time, created man in His image and declared that it was not good for him to be alone.[99] Man had needs that were not being met by his relationship with God or with God's creation. Man needed community—human community. Man was needy. Sometimes we look at our neediness as a weakness or even as a sin. The identification and statement of man's neediness recorded in Genesis 2 precedes Man's sin that occurs in Genesis 3. Neediness is part of our God-given make-up and it is designed to drive us into relationship, into community.

Of course, true to form, Adam was clueless about his neediness. (Are there men out there who got married because they knew they had emotional needs that needed to be met? I didn't think so.) In the second chapter of Genesis, just after God says that it is not good for Adam to be alone, He asks Adam to name all of the animals. At first glance, this seems a bit out of place in the narrative. However, as usual, God knows what He is doing. Adam names the animals that come before him in pairs.

> *Neediness is part of our God-given make-up and it is designed to drive us into relationship, into community.*

I don't know how many pairs walked before him before he realized there was no "other" for him.[100] God knew that Adam would not fully enter in to the community that he created him for unless he knew he needed it. As soon as Adam had this realization, God was ready to put him into a relationship. So God, the God that lived in intimate relationship, the God that created a needy man, created community. He caused the man to sleep, took a rib from his side, made a woman and brought her to Adam.[101] *Ba-da-bing, ba-da-bang*—community!

Now would be a good time for us to pause before we describe this community any further to make sure that each of us is aware of our own need for community. As we talked about choosing honesty in Chapter 5, was there a part of you that longed for someone close enough with whom you could be completely honest, someone who would understand your journey and support you unconditionally? This is a longing for community, and like the desire for life that is in us; it is God-given.

How was this community supposed to work? Both the man and the woman depended on God to meet their needs. The three walked together in the Garden in the cool of the day. Sometimes God met their needs directly and sometimes he used the other person to meet their needs. Larry Crabb in his book, *The Marriage Builder*, describes the intimacy of this first community (marriage) as a ". . . relationship between husband and wife in which both partners turn individually to the Lord in complete dependence upon Him for the satisfaction of their . . . needs and turn to each other in mutual commitment to . . . give themselves to one another to be used according to God's purposes in each other's lives . . . ."[102] Dependence on God, commitment to minister to each other; this is how true community works, this is how intimacy develops. Notice the chart below. As each person in the relationship depends on God and allows Him to use them to minister to the needs of others, the relationship is drawn closer and closer together. Intimacy!

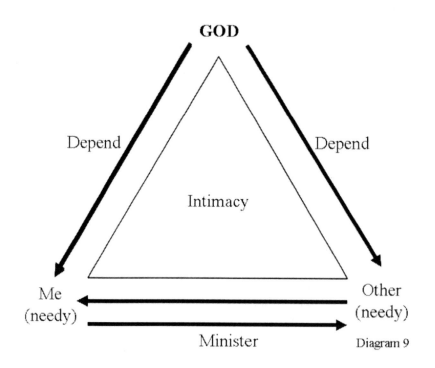

Diagram 9

This model for community must follow these guidelines in order to work properly:

1. We cannot try to get life out of the other person.
2. We cannot expect the other person to meet our needs fully or be the source of our life.
3. We must be aware of the needs of the other person.
4. We must communicate our needs to the other person.
5. We must be willing to go to the Lord when the other person disappoints us, instead of putting up a wall, attacking or retreating.

True community worked perfectly in the Garden of Eden. Adam and Eve knew that their life was dependent on God, not on each other. They were aware that it was really God who was meeting all of their needs. They also recognized they were sometimes the channel God used to minister

Dependence on God, commitment to minister to each other; this is how true community works, this is how intimacy develops.

to the needs of the other. The three of them (God, Adam, and Eve) took walks together in the Garden and did not argue about which path to take, complain about the insects, or bad-mouth their mother-in-law. Does that mean we need to all get naked and find a lush green garden? No. (I can sense your disappointment.) True community worked in the Garden of Eden because Adam and Eve were choosing life at this point. They were not broken, so their relationship was not broken. They were living in connection with the Father and in the center of the Life Chart. They had everything they needed to make community work. When we allow Christ to bring healing to our broken places and live in the center of the Life Chart, we can enjoy true community as well.

It sounds so good, so healthy, so balanced, and so simple. Why is this so hard for us? Why do so many marriages end in divorce, so many churches split, and so many families end up estranged from each other? Why do we struggle with authentic relationships? Why does true community seem a rare commodity in our day? The answer: sin. When Adam and Eve chose death instead of life, their fellowship with God was broken. They were left with just each other. To compound the problem, without God in the picture, they began to focus on themselves and their own needs instead of each other and God. They became self-focused. This explains why they were embarrassed about their bodies (though they had been naked all along) and sewed fig leaves to hide from each other. They were no longer moving toward each other in intimacy; they were moving away from each other into isolation, into hiding. The blaming that follows when God addresses them shows that a part of their positive identity had been shattered. Their sense of community was broken by an inability to really trust each other. Not only had they become self-focused, they had become self-protective. *Eve, why did you give me this fruit to eat? Adam, why didn't you stop me from eating the fruit?* Broken trust yields broken relationships.

Can we see how in our own story, sin and wounds have disrupted true community? Without God as the ultimate source of life and identity, we quickly learn that we cannot trust these precious parts of ourselves to others. They are not capable of giving us life or providing our identity. We become self-focused (*Who is going to meet my needs?*) and self-protective (*I am not going to let them hurt me again.*). Both of these things destroy authentic community and leave us walled off from others. We have lost our ability to trust.

Our response to this broken community varies depending on how we deal with our sin and wounds. Some live in the identity of the "shamed" self, bearing all of the labels and lies that flow out of their sin or wound (the right-hand side of the Life Chart). If we respond this way, we refuse to put forth the effort to create a false self that is more socially acceptable. This shame drives us into isolation. We don't have broken relationships; we have no real relationships at all. We keep our walls tall and thick and refuse to let others in, believing they cannot be trusted and probably don't really care about us. Often isolation results in deeper shame and addictive responses to soothe our loneliness and counteract our bitterness.

Andy Comiskey, in his curriculum entitled, *Living Waters*, says that, ". . . man out of fellowship with God bends toward men."[103] Some people, particularly those who tend to blame other people for their brokenness, turn toward narcissism. Since they cannot trust anyone, they will only trust themselves. When we respond this way, we create an image of ourselves to hide behind and through which we can interpret life (the false self on the left-hand side of the Life Chart). Most of our relationships are entered into for our benefit alone or for what we can get out of them. We struggle with authority because the rules of others do not always benefit us (it's not fair). This narcissism is not always driven by self-love, but often by a deep self-hatred masked by the false self of narcissism. Relationships usually do not last or do not become deep because we are so self-focused and self-protective that we cannot genuinely care about others.

Still others, particularly those who tend to blame themselves for their brokenness (self-contempt), turn toward relational idolatry or co-dependency which we described in a previous chapter. "In short, idolatrous relationships are based on the belief that another person can really make one whole."[104] If this is the way we respond to our sin and wounds, we believe that we are weak, and we need another to lean on to fix us or to take care of us (the false self). Our relationships are imbalanced and may even end up abusive. We may believe that because of our sin and wounds, we don't deserve to be treated well anyway. The unresolved shame can even convince us that we deserve the abusive treatment, and we continue in difficult relationships and lose a sense of who we really are. Many times the idolatrous relationship turns strongly to the sexual aspect. Meeting someone else's sexual needs gives a sense of power that the powerless person desperately needs. This can lead to an addictive, never satisfied, sexual addiction with no regard for health or self.

Whether we lean toward isolation, narcissism or relational idolatry, the fact is that authentic community, the kind we were created to experience, cannot be realized. As we saw earlier, authentic community happens in the center section of the Life Chart, in the place of LIFE. This is why choosing community is a life choice; it moves us back into the direction of intimate relationship with God.

The first step in choosing the direction of genuine community is confession. This confession is not confession to God, which was part of choosing honesty, forgiveness, and surrender. This time we are confessing to our brothers and sisters, our fellow strugglers, and the members of our community. Dietrich Bonhoeffer, a man deeply committed to God and community writes, "A man who confesses his sins in the presence of a brother or sister knows that he is no longer alone with himself; he experiences the presence of God in the reality of another person."[105] As demonstrated by Adam and Eve hiding, sin demands isolation. While living in unconfessed sin, true community is not experienced. Confession, transparency, and accountability are the watchword characteristics of true community. Scripture clearly instructs us to "confess your sins to each other and pray for each other so that you may be healed."[106]

The honesty with which we approach each other in community and the time that we spend together forms a bond and begins to communicate God's unconditional love to each other through human mouths and hands.

After the initial confession, a choice to be honest with the members of the community seals the bond of intimacy. As we become real with one another in community that is founded upon intimate communion with God, we learn and grow from the strengths and weaknesses of the others in community, as iron sharpens iron.[107] The honesty with which we approach each other in community and the time that we spend together forms a bond and begins to communicate God's unconditional love to each other through human mouths and hands. This is experiencing life together. This is what we were created to experience.

My goodness, Bob, isn't this risky? Yes, there is always the risk of being hurt by another when we share our journey, and so we exercise the wisdom of God in those we include in our true community. However, the risk is put in true perspective for us because we know that we are getting life from the Father (who will never reject us) and regardless of what others may say, we are accepted by Him. Living in the identity of the Father takes the power out of others' reactions to us.

We need this honest and transparent community of confession and accountability in order to experience, enjoy, and celebrate the life that God has given us. Remember, God created us to enjoy and need community. When King Solomon, one of the wisest men that has ever lived, wrote a book about life and its pitfalls he said,

> "Two are better than one, because they have a good return for their work; If one falls down, his friend can help him up. But pity the man who falls and has no one to help him up! Also, if two lie down together, they will keep warm. But how can one keep warm alone? Though one may be overpowered, two can defend themselves. A cord of three strands is not quickly broken."[108]

We need each other!

As I moved through my recovery process, community became extremely important to me. Each person who became a part of my support team or authentic community played a vital role in my healing. Bob, the leader of the recovery ministry, was the one who encouraged me to keep moving even when I wanted to quit. The members of my small group who struggled with the same issues as I, felt my pain and prayed for me. My wife Terri chose to find her life in the Father so that she could live with me through my struggles and not be co-dependent. My dear friend Doris became a source of regular encouragement and unconditional love. My friend Don, even knowing all that I struggled with, showed up on my porch at 4:00 in the morning to help me deliver newspapers and pray with me. My counselor Al held me accountable and pushed me to question the system in which I grew up. Jay, my first real buddy, went fishing with me, played racquetball with me, and cared about me. These were all just normal people, but I chose to invite them into my life. They accepted me and became my community. None of them were perfect, but because I was learning to find my life in the Father and not in others, they were free to be imperfect and so was I.

This authentic community is also a reflection of Christ in us. The love of God is deep, unconditional, and is received at the moment of salvation. This love was forever proven to us at the cross, where God gave His Son to die in our place. When we receive this love, it is natural for it to flow from us to others in genuine, caring ways. As we lean into this love of God, we love others. Peter put it this way, "Now that you have purified yourselves by obeying the truth so that you have sincere love for your brothers, love one another deeply, from the heart."[109] Let love flow!

This chapter on choosing community cannot be complete without some mention of the role of the church. In a very real way, the church is our community. The spirit of Christ that lives in us and in every other believer connects us together in ways that call for genuine community. Keep in mind that when we use the word "church" we are not talking about the building or the meeting time, but the actual believers themselves; they are our community. When the church meets together, it should be viewed as an opportunity for God to speak to us directly and through community. The church meeting is not an end in itself; it is a means. No favor with God is gained by attending. The benefit comes in the connection with God and community that takes place as we "come together." The writer of the book of Hebrews put it this way, "Let us consider how we may spur one another on toward love and good deeds. Let us not give up meeting together, as some are in the habit of doing, but let us encourage one another— and all the more as you see the Day approaching."[110]

As we begin to make this life choice, it is important that we move forward wisely. We have been holding our cards tightly to our chest for a long time. It is unwise for us to invite someone into our lives by laying down all of our cards at once. Wisdom would lead us to lay down one card, see how they respond, and then make our choice about moving forward based on that response. Begin to pray now about who the Father may have you invite into your life and be fully open to the unexpected companions He may bring your way. As our broken parts are healed and we live in the middle of the Life Chart, we can choose community. We can choose to break free from isolation, narcissism, and relational idolatry to embrace genuine community through confession, honesty, and spending time together. Choose community!

Chapter 11—Questions to Ponder

1. Look back over the areas of brokenness in your life that you have begun to deal with as you "choose life." How have these areas of brokenness affected your relationships?

2. What basic needs are you aware of that you long to have filled in community? Do you see these needs as sinful or weak?

3. How has broken trust impacted your ability to move into community?

4. Have you experienced authentic community? If so, describe it. If not, why not?

5. Is there someone you can begin to pray with who will be the beginning of a healthy, authentic community? Write his or her name here and pray that the Lord would lead you in this new relationship.

CHAPTER 12

Choose Worship

∽

Cultivating a heart of worship frees my heart to receive the love and instruction from the Father.

Our hearts have been taken captive, walled off and shut down by the sin, wounds, and shame we have experienced, then walled off by the coping mechanisms and addictions we have developed. As we lay all of these things aside by choosing surrender and allowing the Spirit of God in us to realign our will with the Father, as we hear His voice affirming who we are, we receive the refreshing grace that forgives our sin and wounds, we begin to experience a connection with the Father in relationship that we have missed. We begin to experience life. As the life flows into us from the Father, our hearts are awakened to this new relationship with Him. Our hearts have been transformed from "deceitful and desperately wicked"[111] to "new"[112] hearts which are clean and good and which long to connect with the Father. The response of the heart to the presence and experience of the Father is called worship.

If not for the ways that we have attempted worship from the place of shame or from the false self in our past, there would be no need for instruction on how to choose worship; it would flow freely from us. My fear is that as you begin to choose worship, you will go back to old ways and ideas that defined it and find it less than the transforming experience with the Father that it was meant to be.

The word *worship* is used over 200 times in the Scriptures. The Old Testament, written in Hebrew, uses several different words for this action. The most common word literally means *to bow down* or *do homage*. It is most often used as a verb describing a response which is both an action and an attitude and emphasizes a position of humility. The New Testament, written in Greek, basically uses one word for worship that literally means to *kiss toward*. It is used to describe the action of a dog as he moves toward his master's hand to show his loyalty and affection. The action (the kiss) is prompted by the attitude (loyalty and affection). In the same way, our actions in worship (the part you see) are prompted by our attitude toward God.

If worship is both an action and an attitude that happens as a response, what is prompting the response? Is it worship music, prayer, a worship leader waving his arms, or a church sanctuary with stained glass windows? In Isaiah 6, the prophet Isaiah recounts his dramatic vision of God. He sees Him sitting on a throne (which speaks of His sovereignty), filling the temple (which speaks of His omnipresence), causing the doorposts to move (which speaks of His power), and sees heavenly creatures continuously proclaiming His holiness. What did Isaiah do? He worshipped. He repented of his sinful state and then offered himself wholly to God ("Hear am I. Send me."). This is worship—the reality and realization of God's presence prompts a heart attitude (love, affection, humility) which prompts an action (praise, surrender, repentance).

> *This is worship—the reality and realization of God's presence prompts a heart attitude which prompts an action.*

This would be a good place for us to pause. Go get your Bible and slowly read Isaiah 6:1-8. Open up your imagination and put yourself in Isaiah's place. Close your eyes and picture God on the throne as Isaiah describes Him. Get lost in His presence. Worship.

In Revelation 1, the Apostle John who is exiled on an island, sees a vision of the risen Christ. He describes what he sees as a vision of Christ as the judge (eyes of fire, feet of bronze, sword in His mouth). John's response is to fall immediately at his feet. Jesus then commands John to write the vision down and John obeys. This is worship. The reality and realization of the presence of God prompted a heart attitude of humility which prompted John to fall down in homage to God and to willingly obey God's command.

Worship then, is a response to the presence of God. When we become truly aware of our connectedness to Him (that connection is life); our response is worship. This worship will take the form of an attitude (humility, love, praise, thankfulness, awe, joy) and an action (bowing, singing, obeying, serving, praying, crying, and laughing). If we are still living as the shamed self, we cannot worship God (on the right-hand side of the Life Chart). The presence of God is veiled by the cloak of shame and the veil of lies and labels that we are wearing. If we are still living as the false self, we cannot worship God (on the left-hand side of the Life Chart). Our ability to experience the presence of God is blocked by the mask to which we cling. It is diffused by the screen of shame which is generated by our attempts to self-medicate (addictions) and make life work on our own (coping mechanisms). Unless we have made the choices for life and moved back into life (the center section of the Life Chart), we cannot worship God.

There is a difference between worshipping God and performing acts of worship. In Isaiah 1, the prophet speaks out against the nation of Israel because they continue to perform acts of worship like sacrifices, burnt offerings, burning incense, celebrating religious holidays, and praying (verses 11-15) while they are living in rebellion against God. Isaiah speaks of their rebellion, their guilt, their wounds (verses 2-6), and their evil deeds (verse 16). After Isaiah exposes the falseness of their worship, he extends an invitation from God for them to come to Him and allow Him to change their sins which are like scarlet and make them white as snow (verse 18). Isaiah tells them that if they choose life they can worship. If not, they can continue to perform acts of worship which are not only rejected by God, but also create a false sense of relationship with God, preventing them from truly experiencing Him.

Let's pause again here and go back to our Bible. Slowly read Isaiah 1. Identify the acts of worship that we have frequently performed without truly connecting to the presence of the Father. Hear His quiet voice asking us for our heart. Worship.

In my own journey, I was guilty of this false worship. When I lived in the shamed self, I spent time at the foot of the cross weeping, crying out to God and wallowing in my self-pity. I was practicing a form of humility that was passive. Acknowledging that I needed help and begging God to fix me, I was unwilling to engage my own will to choose grace, forgiveness, and truth. This was not worship but performance, a fleshly attempt to invoke God's pity for my circumstance, impress those around me, and try to manipulate God to intervene supernaturally.

When I lived in the power of the false self, I learned how to perform in worship. Using the gift of singing that the Father had given me, I performed worship songs for the praise of men and used the affirmation to keep me going. There was an emotion in me during this worship, but it was not an emotion of humility before the Lord. It did not prompt me to surrender to Him in confession and repentance.

Because worship is both an attitude and an action it involves emotion, volition, feeling, and choice. In fact, worship involves all that we are in response to all that God is. I like the definition of worship recorded by William Temple, Archbishop of Canterbury (1942-44):

> "Both for perplexity and for dulled conscience the remedy is the same; sincere and spiritual worship. For worship is the submission of all our nature to God. It is the quickening of conscience by His holiness; the nourishment of mind by His truth; the purifying of imagination by His beauty; the opening of the heart to His love; the surrender of will to His purpose—and all of this gathered up in adoration, the most selfless emotion of which our nature is capable and therefore the chief remedy for that self-centeredness which is our original sin and the source of all actual sin. Yes—worship in spirit and truth is the way to the solution of perplexity and to the liberation from sin.[113]

As you become aware of God's presence, has your spirit been convicted of unholy living? Has your mind rejoiced in the knowledge of His truth? Has your imagination been awakened by the beauty of His handiwork? Has your heart overflowed with the experience of His love? Has your will bowed to His will? This is worship. It is a response of all that I am to all that God is.

I would be remiss if I did not mention the physical aspect of worship. The worship experiences of both Isaiah and John previously noted involved a physical aspect. Isaiah felt the touch of God on his lips and John physically fell on his face. Both entered into worship not only spiritually and emotionally, but also physically. Fully entering into a worship experience does involve our physical bodies. The Bible speaks of kneeling before the Lord, lying prostrate before Him, lifting our hands to Him, and even dancing before Him as responses to His presence.

In the beginning stages of my healing process, it was difficult for me to enter physically into worship. There were three reasons for this struggle. First, I was raised in a Baptist church where we sat on our hands and sang the hymns with no physical display. Years of training in that worship experience left me physically detached from God's presence. Second, because of the abuse and the lies I believed, I hated my body (a by-product of self-contempt). I did not see myself as physically masculine enough and thus tended to shun any focus on the physical. Third, because of my sexual addiction, any focus on the physical quickly became sensual and distracted me from any focus on spiritual things. I simply could not enter into worship with my body in any way.

Fortunately for me, the Lord knew the importance of breaking down this stronghold in my life. My recovery group was very charismatic and free in their worship style. People were lifting their hands, clapping, dancing and jumping up and down, kneeling, and even twirling flags during the worship experience. Not only that, they used water as a symbol of cleansing and oil as a symbol of the power of the Holy Spirit. I not only stood stoically during the worship experience, but I refused to allow anyone to anoint me with water or oil. *Leave my body out of this!*

As the Lord began to set me free from my sin, wounds, shame and guilt, it became easier for me to lift my hands, clap to the music, and physically enter into worship. However, I still refused the water and oil. I finished the first 36 weeks of this recovery program without allowing anyone to touch me physically with these elements. A month after the completion of this phase of my recovery, I found myself at a Promise Keepers Rally at RFK Stadium in Washington, DC. The worship music was incredible, and I was caught up in the community of thousands of men praising the Lord. I lifted my hands, cried, knelt, and even danced a little as I worshipped the Lord. As the worship band continued, a dark cloud moved over the stadium and a torrential downpour began. The praise band kept playing. Many people ran for cover, but others just lifted their hands and let the rain soak them. I stayed in my place, continued to sing and praise the Lord, and entered emotionally into the worship. As the tears and rain streamed down my face, the Father spoke to me . . . *I got you with the water!* If I wouldn't accept the physical symbolic act of cleansing using water from men, God would have to do it Himself. It was a powerful experience of worship and broke down some pretty thick walls, bringing even more healing to the area of self-hatred and self-contempt in my life.

Having shared these thoughts about worship let me caution you. Don't try to over-analyze worship. There is always a sense of wonder accompanying the awareness of the presence of God. In Luke 4 and 5 when Jesus performed miracles, the people were amazed and filled with wonder. In Acts 2 when the disciples stood up in Jerusalem and preached in many languages that they had never studied, the people were amazed. The presence of God is completely unexplainable; it is a mystery and should cause us to wonder. Warren Wiersbe puts it this way in *Real Worship*.

> "The trouble is that wonder is a rare ingredient. You do not often find it present in most modern worship. After all, what is there to wonder about? Why should there be any mystery in the worship experience of the average congregation? We know all about God, because we know our Bible so well. We study; we listen to sermons, in person and by means of cassette; we read books that explain what God and the Christian life are all about. We have outlined the Bible, analyzed God's attributes, and charted the ages. What is there to elicit our wonder? . . . The church today is imperiled by what it thinks it understands."[114]

Don't try to understand all that God is doing as you enter into worship. Just enter in. Participate. Celebrate. Experience his presence with a sense of wonder and awe.

Since life is this connectedness to the Father and we get our true identity from Him, worship is an experience of transformation. Paul says that as we reflect the Lord's glory in His presence, we are changed from the inside out. We begin to understand our identity in Christ better and can allow His life to flow out through us. Our service to God is changed from a duty or an attempt to earn favor with Him and becomes a response to who He is and what He has done. It isn't forced or drudgery, it is free and celebrated.

When Samuel, the Old Testament prophet, was moving off of the scene and transferring leadership of the nation of Israel to their first King, Saul, he uttered words of parting advice. He said, "Be sure to fear the Lord and serve him faithfully with all your heart; consider what great things He has done for you."[115] This was a reminder about the importance of worship. It contained emotion (fear), action (serve), involved the whole person (with all your heart), and was a response (consider what He has done for you).

Choose worship—not disconnected acts of worship—but true worship from the heart as a response to the presence of God in your life!

Chapter 12—Questions to Ponder

1. By using this chapter and your own experiences, write a definition of worship.

2. Note all of the aspects of the worship experience related by John in Revelation 4.

3. Contrast the worship experiences in your own life from the three positions on the Life Chart:

   a) From the shamed self –

   b) From the false self—

   c) From the true self –

4. Have you worshipped God with all that you are? Give an example of each from your own experience.

   a) Worship that included conviction of sin –

   b) Worship that included rejoicing in the truth –

   c) Worship that awakened your imagination to beauty –

   d) Worship that overwhelmed you with His love –

   e) Worship that bowed your will to His desire –

   f) Worship that included your physical body—

5. Formulate a prayer sharing your desire with the Father for Him to draw you into a transforming experience of worship. Pray this prayer regularly.

CHAPTER 13

Choose Intimacy

✑

Moving toward an intimate relationship with God through
discipleship frees me from empty religion and isolation.

Intimacy, knowing and being known at the deepest level of who we are, is a longing built into every man and woman. In the quietness of the Garden of Eden, there was intimacy between Adam and Eve. They were "naked and unashamed;"[116] i.e., physically, emotionally, or spiritually unguarded and able to share on the deepest level their ambitions, desires, fears, and secrets with no shame. This is true intimacy and this is a deep longing in each of us; to be connected, accepted, understood, and loved.

I realize that for some (the majority men), intimacy is mostly linked with the physical and sexual relationship with another. If we think of intimacy as "naked and unashamed" it makes sense that this would be a part of our thinking. The sexual relationship *is* a form of intimacy and can be the fullest expression of intimacy from person to person, providing that the connection includes the heart and spirit, not just the body. Unresolved issues, anger, fear, bitterness, and pain are obstacles to relational intimacy on the physical level, just as they are obstacles to relational intimacy with God on a spiritual level.

Through the life choices that we have walked through in this book, we have removed many of the obstacles to intimacy with God. We have established the possibility of experiencing that intimacy through the person of Christ. Because of the grace and complete forgiveness that Christ offers through His sacrifice on the cross, we can lay down all of our shame, guilt, labels, and lies and stand as a righteous child of the Father with nothing to hide and nothing to hold back (naked and unashamed) because we are fully defined by Him. It is vital to recognize that any hesitation in making the previous life choices will limit our ability to stand naked and unashamed before the Father. As we move toward intimacy in this discussion, any remnant of shame, guilt, unforgiveness, coping mechanisms, contempt, addiction, or masks will become an obstacle that stands in the way of choosing intimacy with God.

Intimacy begins with desire. Most of our choices, actions, and behaviors flow out of desire. The person who struggles with addiction cries out in desperation, *Why do I keep doing this over and over again?* The answer is desire. We act because we want to act. We move toward what we desire. The problem is that the surface desires of our flesh often rule what drives us because we are not connected to the deepest desires within us. Richard Foster, in his classic work the *Celebration of Discipline,* says that "superficiality is the curse of our age."[117] There is a depth to us that longs to connect with the depth of who God is. Scripture says that "deep calls to deep."[118] However, the shallow desires of our flesh are calling out to be satisfied by the shallow pleasures of this world. The voices are so much louder, the connections more familiar, and therefore perceived as so much easier. Our sin, addictions, coping mechanisms, flesh patterns, and shame have prevented us from touching those deeper desires of our heart that would lead us to intimacy with God and made it easier for us to settle for lesser attachments. Think about how much easier it is, at times, to get on the computer for another mindless game, watch another episode of CSI, or eat another bowl of ice cream than it is to purposely get alone with God to hear Him speak through His Word. As we surrender these lesser attachments to God, the deeper desires begin to rise in need of connection with the Father. Raw desire for intimacy with the Father lies in the deepest part of who we are and will not be accessed if we continue to live on the surface of our being.

Intimacy, knowing and being known at the deepest level of who we are, is a longing built into every man and woman.

This move to deeper desire requires us to get in touch with our hearts, the source of our desire. As we have dealt with our sin and wounds and embraced the truth of who we really are in Christ, we begin to realize that our hearts are good. As we surrender our masks, shame, and coping mechanisms, we begin to realize that we don't need to build walls around our hearts. We don't have to fear our emotions. We can trust our hearts. We can feel. We can feel deeply. We can love. We can love deeply. We can be passionate. We can be deeply passionate! We can connect our hearts to the heart of God and the hearts of others.

In the early part of my recovery process, the period that I call *the time of white knuckling*, I knew that I needed to deny the shallow desires that had become addictive which were destroying my relationships and disrupting life. I had always been a passionate person and felt things deeply. My addiction to the feelings associated with my sexual sin was strong and passionate. My earliest success in stopping the sinful patterns came when I shut down my heart and passions altogether. Not feeling, I thought was the way to shut down these shallow desires. On one level it worked; I was able to stop acting out in sexual ways. However, on another level, I took a step backwards. I was also unable to connect on a deeper level with God and the significant people in my life because I just stopped feeling. I was not in touch with my heart.

While for that short period, I do believe that the *white knuckling* helped me in my journey, ultimately God's plan for healing and life does not mean that we shut down our hearts. Jesus sought to connect with the hearts of the people to whom He ministered. For example, one day Jesus was leaving a particular city, surrounded by a crowd of people, when he heard someone calling out loudly from the side of the road, "Jesus, Son of David, have mercy on me." Jesus heard the pain and desperation in this man's voice and He called for the man to be brought to Him. As he approached, it was apparent that the man was blind. Surely, since Jesus had healed others who were blind, it was obvious what the man wanted. Regardless of how apparent it seemed, Jesus still asked the question, "What do you want me to do for you?" Jesus' question was less about information and more about giving the blind man a chance to speak out of the deepest desire in his heart. His response was simple, "Rabbi, I want to see." Jesus allowed the man to connect with the deepest part of his heart before He ministered healing to him.[119]

In a similar story, one that we referred to in an earlier chapter, Jesus was in Jerusalem and He walked through the sheep gate onto a series of porches that surrounded a pool. There was a prevailing belief that on occasion, an angel would come down and stir the waters of the pool. After the stirring, the first disabled person who entered the waters would be healed. Because of this belief, the porches were always filled with broken people. As Jesus stepped onto the porches, He approached a man who had been paralyzed for 38 years. Again, it was obvious why the man was there and what he wanted. But this did not keep Jesus from asking the question, "Do you want to get well?" Jesus wanted the man to connect with the deep desire of his heart before He ministered to him.[120] *Do you want to get well?* Let's think about that question for a moment. I would assume that the answer is yes. (Not only did you pick up this book, but you have made it to chapter 13.) But have you really connected to the deep desires of your heart? Could you express them clearly to God if He were to ask you? Can you see how the shallow desires of the flesh have robbed you of the ability to access these deeper desires?

God built deep desire into us and He longs to satisfy that desire. "Delight yourself in the Lord and he will give you the desires of your heart."[121] He does not promise to give us the shallow desires of our flesh, but He longs to give us the deepest desires of our hearts. (I used to read this verse and think, relaxing day on the beach, deep tissue massage, a large screen TV, and remote.)

God built deep desire into us and He longs to satisfy that desire.

As we remove the walls, barriers, and partitions we've erected around our hearts through the various life choices, we need our hearts to come alive and reconnect us with our deepest desires. Dealing with our past issues has torn down the old walls. What will awaken our hearts to this deep desire? Love. The heart was made to love. Jesus revealed that the greatest commandments were to love God with all your heart and to love others as yourself.[122] As we make these life choices, we grow in our security in His love and our fear of rejection decreases. Now we are more willing to open our hearts to God and others; as we do, we are changed. A sequence has developed that may look something like this:

1. Truth convinces us that we are secure in the Father.
2. Healing breaks down the walls around our hearts.
3. Our hearts become more open to love.
4. Love awakens desire.
5. Desire drives us to intimacy.

This was illustrated for me this past summer on our beach vacation. As I sat in my chair under the umbrella, relaxing and enjoying the breeze, I noticed a man walking toward the water. He had tatoos up and down both arms, bulging muscles, broad shoulders, and was chiseled with an ugly scar on the left side. He reminded me of someone who could be a bouncer in a club or the muscle for a mobster. It was obvious that his life had led him to some pretty rough places and he was not someone to make angry. He went to the water's edge, knelt down, and turned to walk back up the beach toward me. Now I could see that he was carrying something. At the end of each of those huge arms, which had undoubtedly decked many a man, hung a large pink bucket filled with water. He carried the water up the beach and set each one down carefully beside two cute petite, playful, blonde-haired girls. I watched as he gently helped them build a sand castle and then took them, one in each arm, down to the ocean to rinse the sand off of their hands. I began to think. What changed this rough and tough "Rambo-type man" into a careful, gentle, and loving father? Love. It was obvious that he had opened up his heart to love these girls and that love had connected him to the deepest part of who he was and . . . he changed. Love had enabled him to get in touch with his deepest desires and had led him into an intimate, loving relationship with his daughters. Do you love deeply? If not, what wall around your heart is keeping you from experiencing the love of God in a deep and profound way?

In our last chapter, we chose worship. Choosing intimacy and choosing worship are very closely related. Worship is a response of adoration and love to the presence of a God of love. Worship allows us to open up our newly healed hearts and express our deep love for Him as we bask in His great love for us. This love can lead us to the same life-transforming changes that I noticed in the man on the beach. We leave behind the things we tried to get life from before and we devote ourselves to a deeper relationship with the One who loves us and is the object of our love. Worship, then, is the life choice that can open up our hearts to our true desire for God and lead us to intimacy with Him.

The change that is brought about by opening up our hearts to the Father (which often happens during worship) is absolutely necessary, because God will not and cannot change to become intimate with us. He has provided the way and extended the means by which we can approach Him. Now we must use His avenue and adjust to draw near to Him. Chuck Swindoll put it this way, "God will never adjust His agenda to fit ours. He will not speed His pace to catch up with ours; we need to slow our pace in order to recover our walk with Him. God will not scream and shout over the noisy clamor; He expects us to seek quietness, where His still small voice can be heard again."[123]

This leads us to discipleship, or the spiritual disciplines. Paul instructed Timothy to train himself to be godly.[124] The word *train* that Paul used is the Greek word from which we get our English word, *gymnasium*. It carries with it the idea of discipline and conditioning. Godly is a word which means to be pious, to revere, or to worship well. It carries with it the idea of being completely devoted to God. According to Paul, there are "exercises" which by repeated, disciplined use, can lead a person toward deeper devotion to God. These exercises are called *spiritual disciplines*.

Spiritual disciplines are activities that are entered into with the express purpose of making more room for God in our lives (opening up our hearts to Him). The practice of spiritual disciplines will not make you more acceptable to God (you are already accepted). They are not laws to be obeyed (that's legalism) but invitations into relationship. The exercises vary and different ones minister to different personalities in more or less profound ways. Simplicity, silence, meditation, prayer, worship, celebration, study, fasting, solitude, confession, submission, and service are among these exercises. Several classic works that describe the practice of these disciplines and their benefits include:

> *Sacred Rhythms* by Ruth Haley Barton
> *Celebration of Discipline* by Richard Foster
> *The Spirit of the Disciplines* by Dallas Willard
> *So, You Want to Be Like Christ?* by Charles Swindoll
> *Spiritual Disciplines Handbook* by Adele Ahlberg Calhoun

While the long list of disciplines and the many instructional books written may lead you to believe that this is a hard thing to learn, the truth is that it is very easy. Practicing the spiritual discipline of solitude simply means regularly getting in a place of quietness and aloneness where all other voices are stilled, and the still small voice of God can be clearly heard. The discipline of prayer is the practice of talking with God regularly and intimately including quiet times where we listen for His voice. The discipline of celebration is allowing ourselves to respond to God's goodness in our lives with utter abandon—no inhibitions. Exploring the disciplines, practicing several, and finding the ones that help to create the most space in your life for this intimacy with God is a great follow-up to reading this book.

Now that we have introduced the disciplines as a pathway to intimacy, I want to go back to the sequence that I introduced earlier in the chapter and insert the disciplines as a part of this journey toward intimacy. The new sequence would look something like this:

1. Truth convinces us that we are secure in the Father.
2. Healing breaks down the walls around our hearts.
3. Our hearts become more open to love.
4. Love awakens desire.
5. Desire drives us to practice the spiritual disciplines.
6. The disciplines create space in our lives for intimacy with the Father.

Training or discipline, though, always has a goal. The Olympic athlete trains for his sport toward a contest with athletes from other nations. The goal of the spiritual disciplines according to the Bible is godliness, full devotion to God. As we focus on the Father and open our hearts to Him, our desire leads us to seek Him more and more. As we seek Him more and more, our self-focus begins to fade, our need

> *The goal of the spiritual disciplines according to the Bible is godliness, full devotion to God.*

to self-protect is diminished as our trust in Him increases, and our focus on Him begins to become the driving factor in our lives. Our desire to isolate from God and others is eliminated. The deep desire to connect with God and others in intimacy is heightened. We are conscious only of Him; we are naked and unashamed in His presence.

Church takes on new meaning as we choose intimacy. We don't see our time at church as attending a worship service, taking a class, or singing some worship songs. Church becomes an opportunity to connect with the Father and with others in a corporate setting. Through worship, our tired hearts open up to His love and goodness. Through preaching and teaching, our hearts and minds receive fresh insight to truth and instruction that feels more like an intimate conversation than a "how-to manual." Through prayer and quietness, we sense the arms of the Father holding us in His lap and whispering in our ears. Through fellowship with others we sense that we are a part of His body, accomplishing His purposes in the world. Good-bye empty religion—hello intimacy!

This process of spiritual transformation is exemplified in King David and is illustrated for us throughout the book of Psalms. David's deep longing and thirst for God resulted in him being the only man in Scripture to be called a man after God's own heart. This is the process that the Apostle Paul alluded to many times in the epistles that he wrote to the churches. He told the believers in Philippi that his greatest desire was to *know Christ*, deeply, experientially, and intimately.

This is the process that I have been involved in since the beginning of my recovery process. As I have studied the disciplines and their power to create space for the Father in my life, I have found that the discipline of solitude is particularly powerful for me. I am a "people person" and am involved in a variety of ministries which keep me in direct interaction with people constantly. As I studied through the gospels, I became aware of how often Jesus got away to spend a time of solitude with the Father. At first my response was one of longing, only with the corresponding realization that my schedule was too busy to allow for such an activity. But Jesus surely was far busier than I am. Although He had a heart for people and longed to meet their needs, His priority was His relationship with the Father. He was never too busy to break from people to sit with His Father. Slowly, I began to practice this discipline. At this point in my life and ministry, I try to get away for 24 hours of solitude once each month. I go to a bed and breakfast, with no phone, no television, only a few people, and just sit with God. It is amazing to me that when the quietness hits, the voice of God and the direction from Him becomes so much clearer. I always return from these times refreshed and recharged, fully connected to the Father and focused on Him. As I put the finishing touches on this chapter, I am participating in a week-long quiet retreat called Sabbath Rest at Selah Ranch in Mt. Vernon, TX. In this quietness I am finding the voice of God directing my thoughts with great clarity. Because of their transforming power, I never look at these times as drudgery; I look forward to them and cherish them. Think of it, the Father loves me so much He wants me to stop everything that I am doing so that He can spend some focused time with me—just me! If the practice of the disciplines begins to feel like a chore, there may be an obstacle that needs to be addressed.

I've been using the word *process* throughout this chapter. The truth is that choosing intimacy is not a one-time choice—we are always choosing intimacy; it is an ongoing process. Yes, I sense that I am so much closer to the Father than I have been and my relationship is so much deeper. But there is more; there is always more. It just keeps getting better.

Choosing intimacy for you will probably involve several things. First, you must consider whether you have been willing to really open your heart to God. Do your times of worship communicate the love relationship that exists between you and the Father? If not, perhaps you need to deal with another obstacle lurking in your heart. Second, you must express the deep desires of your heart. Put yourself in the place of the blind man or the paralyzed man and hear Jesus asking you, "What is it that you really want?" Journal and pray the desires of your heart and allow the Father to turn them toward Him. Third, you must explore the spiritual disciplines and allow God to lead you to a practice that will expand the space in your life for Him and draw you closer into His embrace. Choose Intimacy!

Chapter 13—Questions to Ponder

1. Have the desires of your flesh so driven your life up to this point that you have not been totally aware of the deeper desires of your heart? Explain.

2. As the walls around your heart are torn down and you receive the love of the Father, write down some thoughts about your deepest desires.

3. Would you be willing to begin to seek the Lord in prayer concerning your deep desires? Write out a short prayer that you can begin praying regularly in your time with the Father.

4. Have you had any experience with spiritual disciplines? Was it positive or negative? Explain.

5. What do you understand to be the goal of the practice of the spiritual disciplines?

6. Circle a spiritual discipline or two that interests you and that you will look into for future growth:

Meditation	Submission
Service	Confession
Worship	Guidance
Celebration	Prayer
Fasting	Study
Solitude	Simplicity

Choose Availability

Remaining open to all of the ways that God may want to use my journey to impact others frees me from self-focus.

As we move into this last chapter, I can hear some of you asking if you are done yet. You want to know if you are ready for the "life certificate." The truth is (and I saved it for this last chapter on purpose), we are never done in this life. We will always have new challenges and circumstances which give us the opportunity to choose life. We will continue to be triggered and have a tendency to revert back to old patterns and need to refresh our life choice. This may sound discouraging; in truth it is encouraging. Just like Adam and Eve, every day for the rest of our earthly journey, we get to choose life. I think that is exciting! To add to the excitement, now that we have made some good life choices, we can actually choose to share life with others. We have something (life) that others need, and we can direct them to the very place (the Father) where they can find it. We can, that is, if we are willing to make this last life choice. Choose availability.

The other day I received a voice mail about a couple who were struggling with their teenager. Their oldest son is 14 and exhibiting signs of rebellion and anger. They had only known him to be a happy, easy-going child and now that puberty had arrived, everything had changed. They wanted to come in and talk with me about what was going on and get some advice. As I listened to the message and evaluated my response, I had several thoughts. I was beginning to parent my fourth teenager, so I did have some experience with this subject. I hadn't been particularly good at handling all of their teenage problems. In fact,

I often felt inadequate in this role. Part of what I had resigned myself to was that each teen was different and since they didn't come with a manual, it was anyone's guess how to deal with them. As I pondered these things, I was definitely leaning toward calling back and telling them that I really felt I had nothing to offer them. But, as I picked up the phone to call, a thought hit me. They weren't asking me to fix the problem or to be an expert—they were just asking me if I was willing to try to help. *Was I willing?* Not *was I competent?* Not *did I have a guaranteed answer?* Not *was I a perfect parent?* But, *was I willing?*

This story perfectly illustrates the major thrust of this life choice. Choosing availability is *not* about how I will *perform* in this "helping" role, but whether or not I am open to *any way that God may use me in the life of others.* As I evaluated the voice mail request and thought about my own inadequacies, I was focusing on self. When I finally picked up the phone and expressed my willingness to meet with them, it was not about what I could offer; it was just about being willing to help them.

The greatest ability that we have to help others is our availability. There are many good rehab clinics, good support groups, and great psychologists in the United States, but none of them do me any good if they are not available. While your credentials to help others may not rise to the level of these resources, your

The greatest ability that we have to help others is our availability.

availability puts you on the front line as a resource to help those who are struggling.

In spite of this discussion on the importance of willingness over adequacy, the truth is that we have more than enough resources to help a fellow struggler. Having chosen life, we have the power of the resurrected Christ in us. We know the truth. We understand grace and forgiveness and its power to set us free. We recognize masks, coping mechanisms, and methods of self-medication. We are equipped to be a healer, a wounded healer, which is the best kind.

I can hear the objections already forming in your mind. *But I am not articulate. I don't know how to counsel someone else.* Whenever I hear these phrases, I think of the song *Love Them Like Jesus* by Casting Crowns. Read the lyrics and identify.

The love of her life is drifting away
Their losing the fight for another day
The life that she's known is falling apart
A fatherless home, a child's broken heart

You're holding her hand
You're straining for words
You're trying to make sense of it all
She's desperate for hope
Darkness clouding her view
And she's looking to you

Just love her like Jesus
Carry her to Him
His yoke is easy
His burden is light
You don't need the answers
To all of life's questions
Just know that He loves her
And stay by her side
Love her like Jesus.

As I think back to some of the people that the Father used in the most powerful way in my recovery, I remember they were not trained professionals. They were people who loved me like Jesus: my wife Terri loved me enough to relinquish me to God and let Him deal with me; my friend Don, who showed up at 4:00 in the morning to deliver newspapers with me and encourage me; and my small group members, who grieved with me over my losses and mistakes and prayed for my healing. Choose to be one of these people in the lives of others. Choose availability.

A second objection that we often use is that even if we are willing, we do not have anything to offer to someone who is struggling. The truth is, the one thing that the Father wants to use the most, we definitely possess—our own journey. While we may look at our past journey as a liability, the Lord can turn it around and use it as an asset in ministering to others. Scripture teaches us that those who love God and are called by Him (those who choose life) have the added benefit that even those things which seem negative to us, God is "working them together for good."[125] When we share our own struggle with someone else who is struggling, it helps them to feel that they are not alone or unique in their problems. When we share our experience of healing or victory, it gives them hope. In this way, even the sin, wounds, masks, and shame that we struggled with are being used by the Father for good.

Bob, the leader of my recovery group, has painfully shared his journey with homosexuality openly with me, holding nothing back. Through his open and honest sharing (without a degree in psychology, the Bible, or counseling), I have found great healing. Now I share my journey through abuse, sexual addiction, and depression with anyone who will listen. From this, I get the tremendous privilege of watching the Father not only heal others but redeem the years I wasted existing apart from real life.

As we share our journey with others, we also share the role that the presence of God played in that journey. Paul told the Christians that lived at Corinth, a city in Greece, that God was the "Father of all compassion and comfort." He soothes us in all of our troubles "So that we can comfort those in any trouble with the comfort we ourselves have received from God."[126] I remember the leader of one of my small groups sharing about how after he came to terms with his addiction, he went through a period where the desire was so strong, he basically had to *white knuckle* it through until the cravings subsided. While he was sharing a weakness and hard spot in his journey, it definitely encouraged me because I was experiencing the same thing and needed to hear that I wasn't *doing it all wrong.*

We cannot underestimate the power of this level of sharing. I will never forget a dear woman who came to join our church several years ago. During the membership interview, she became a little nervous and said she had something she needed to share with me. With much shame, she admitted that she was currently taking an anti-depressant because she had been unable to get complete victory over her struggle with depression. She clearly felt that this labeled her as spiritually inadequate. When I shared with her that I had been taking anti-depressants for the past 10 years, she let out a deep sigh of relief. She wasn't the only one! As we continued to talk, we discovered we took the exact same medication, and I offered to share mine with her if she ever ran out and couldn't get to the pharmacy. Now that is Pastoral Care!

When the Apostle Paul struggled with a weak area of his life, he begged the Lord on three different occasions to take the struggle from him (my own experience was more like 300 times). In the end, he was reminded by the Father that His grace was enough for him and that God's power was actually more effective through his weaknesses than through his strengths. Personally, I am not a good athlete, handyman, or weight lifter, but I have a strong gift of teaching. God uses this gift in tremendous ways, but if you ask those who sit under my ministry, they will tell you that the transparency about my weaknesses is more powerful than my teaching. God can use your journey. Choose availability.

Of course, the goal is to have this availability flow out of your life choices. It is possible that some choose availability as a form of penance or "earning points" with God. This violates the whole paradigm of *choose life*. The biblical model of how choosing availability flows out of life choices is found in Isaiah 6, which we looked at in an earlier

A true experience with God is absolutely necessary if we want to be available to Him totally.

chapter, where the prophet Isaiah is called to serve God. The first thing that happens in this chapter is that Isaiah sees the Lord. He comes face to face with His holiness, His power, and His presence. A true experience with God is absolutely necessary if we want to be available to Him totally. As Isaiah reacted to God's presence, he was immediately aware of his own sinfulness. He repented (chose honesty) and was cleansed by God (chose grace, chose forgiveness). As soon as Isaiah received this cleansing, he heard the voice of God calling, "Whom shall I send? And who will go for us?" I believe that the Lord was calling all along, but until Isaiah had chosen honesty, grace, and forgiveness, he could not hear the voice of the Lord. As you reflect on the Life Chart, remember that the sin and wounds block our communion with the Father. When these are removed by choosing honesty, grace and forgiveness, the voice of the Father is heard with clarity. When Isaiah did hear the voice of God, his first response was to choose surrender, "Here am I. Send me!" He immediately became available. His availability flowed out of his life choices.

I believe that our experience will be the same as Isaiah's. As we move through the life choices, we will clearly hear the Father calling us to make ourselves available for Him to use in helping others on their journey to deeper relationship with Him. If we are willing, He will use us.

How will God use us? Will we have to write a book, share our whole story on the Oprah Winfrey show, or spill our guts from the pulpit at church? There is no formula for how the Lord will use our healing journey in the lives of others. We need to become observant and conscious of people that God brings into our lives who may need healing or brought along side for our own encouragement. We can intentionally involve ourselves in a recovery-type ministry. We can take on a ministry of encouragement to others through sending cards or visiting in the hospital. We can join a prayer team. If we are willing and available, God will open the door and we will know when He wants us to share parts of our journey. Choose availability!

Chapter 14—Questions to Ponder

1. As you think about the possibility of the Lord using you to help others who are struggling, what objections enter your mind?

2. Can you think of some people that the Lord has used to help you on your journey who were not professionals but simply fellow strugglers? Name them.

3. II Corinthians 1:3-4 talks about comforting others with the same comfort that we have received. List four truths that the Lord has taught you in your recovery that you could share with others.

4. Read I Corinthians 12. How has the Father uniquely gifted you to minister to others?

Appendix 1

Appendix 1: Feelings associated with Sin and Wounds

Wounded (Hurt)
Rejected
Disappointed
Let-down
Uncared-for

Attacked
Put-down (Degraded)
Condemned
Judged
Persecuted
Punished
Like I was on trial

Controlled
Imposed upon
Manipulated
Intimidated
Pressured
Dominated
Like a slave

Boxed-in
Trapped
Like a prisoner
Caught in a no-win
  situation
Caught in the middle

Deceived (Misled)
Lied to
Betrayed
Cheated (Tricked)

Taken for a ride
Suckered
Gullible
Like a fool
Stupid (Dumb)

Foolish
Silly
Ridiculous
Ridiculed
Like I don't fit in
Like I don't belong
Different

Like something is
  wrong with me
Out of place
Strange (Odd)
Weird
Disconnected
Left-out

Excluded
Ignored
Alienated
Isolated (Pushed Away)
Like a stranger
Lonely

Abandoned
Alone
Cut-off
Distant

Inferior
Inadequate
Inept
Like a failure
Impotent

Incompetent
Like I can't be trusted
Unreliable
Not dependable
Screwed-up
Insane (Crazy)
At wits end

Exasperated
Worn-out (Tired)
Wiped-out
Burned-out
Overwhelmed
Exhausted
Weak (Dead)

Like I was dying
Frustrated
Confused
Shocked (Surprised)
Paralyzed (Stunned)
Numb

Discouraged
Defeated
Dejected
Despair

Appendix 1, continued

Destroyed	Abused	Skeptical
Shattered (Crushed)	Raped	Untrusting
Misunderstood	Victimized	Jealous
Falsely Accused	Tortured	Envious
Slandered	Guilty	Covetous
Anxious	Evil (Wicked)	Selfish
Nervous (Tense)	Ashamed (Shame)	Embarrassed
Uptight (Restless)	Cheap	Humiliated
Apprehensive	Dirty (Unclean)	Self-conscious
Defensive	Immoral	Unsure (Uncertain)
On guard	Like a bad person	Doubts about myself
Afraid (Fearful)	Disgusting	Like a hypocrite
Worried (Scared)	Sick to my stomach	Phony
Threatened	Unloved	Irritated
Petrified	Unlovable	
Frightened	Unworthy	
Out of control	Unlikable	
Distressed	Unimportant	
Distraught (No hope)	Worthless	
Hopeless	Useless (Not needed)	
Helpless	Insignificant	
Like giving up	Not Respected	
Vulnerable	Mean	
Insecure	Unkind	
Unprotected	Callous (Uncaring)	
Exposed	Unapproachable	
Naked	Like a monster	
Defenseless	Indifferent	
Violated	Cynical	

Appendix 2

Appendix 2: Who I am in Christ—My new identity

"The more you reaffirm who you are in Christ, the more your behavior will begin to reflect your true identity!"
(From *Victory Over the Darkness* by Dr. Neil Anderson)

I am accepted . . .

John 1:12	I am God's child.
John 15:15	As a disciple, I am a friend of Jesus Christ.
Romans 5:1	I have been justified.
1 Corinthians 6:17	I am united with the Lord, and I am one with Him in spirit.
1 Corinthians 6:19-20	I have been bought with a price and I belong to God.
1 Corinthians 12:27	I am a member of Christ's body.
Ephesians 1:3-8	I have been chosen by God and adopted as His child.
Colossians 1:13-14	I have been redeemed and forgiven of all my sins.
Colossians 2:9-10	I am complete in Christ.
Hebrews 4:14-16	I have direct access to the throne of grace through Jesus Christ.

I am secure...

Romans 8:1-2	I am free from condemnation.
Romans 8:28	I am assured that God works for my good in all circumstances.
Romans 8:31-39	I am free from any condemnation brought against me and I cannot be separated from the love of God.

2 Corinthians 1:21-22	I have been established, anointed and sealed by God.
Colossians 3:1-4	I am hidden with Christ in God.
Philippians 1:6	I am confident that God will complete the good work He started in me.
Philippians 3:20	I am a citizen of heaven.
2 Timothy 1:7	I have not been given a spirit of fear but of power, love and a sound mind.
1 John 5:18	I am born of God and the evil one cannot touch me.

I am significant...

John 15:5	I am a branch of Jesus Christ, the true vine, and a channel of His life.
John 15:16	I have been chosen and appointed to bear fruit.
1 Corinthians 3:16	I am God's temple.
2 Corinthians 5:17-21	I am a minister of reconciliation for God.
Ephesians 2:6	I am seated with Jesus Christ in the heavenly realm.
Ephesians 2:10	I am God's workmanship.
Ephesians 3:12	I may approach God with freedom and confidence.
Philippians 4:13	I can do all things through Christ, who strengthens me.

References

1 Genesis 2:7

2 Genesis 2:24

3 Genesis 3:4

4 Genesis 3:5

5 Proverbs 14:12

6 Genesis 3:15

7 Genesis 4:1-8

8 Genesis 4:12

9 Hebrews 10:1-4

10 Hebrews 10:8-14

11 John 1:29

12 John 10:10

13 John 11:25

14 John 14:6

15 Ephesians 2:8-9

16 John 14:6

17 Genesis 2:18

18 Genesis 2:20

19 Genesis 3:8

20 Matthew 11:28

21 Luke 13:3

22 Matthew 9:12-13

23 Romans 6:6

24 Galatians 2:20

25 Ezekiel 36:26-27

26 Romans 8:15-25

27 John 14:6

28 Hebrews 4:16

29 John 3:16

30 I John 5:12

31 John 11:26

32 Feldmoth, Joanne Ross & Finley, Midge Wallace, *We Weep for Ourselves and For our Children.* (New York: Harper Collins Publishing, 1990), pp. 9-11.

33 Genesis 1:26

34 Genesis 2:18

35 Genesis 1:27

36 Romans 3:23; Isaiah 59:2

37 John 8:44

38 Smedes, Lewis, *Shame and Grace.* (New York: Harper Collins Publishing, 1993), p. 6.

39 Genesis 3:7

40 Genesis 3:9-11

41 I John 1:9

42 James 5:16

43 Romans 3:23

44 I John 1:5-9

45 II Samuel 11, 12

46 Buchanan, Mark, *The Rest of God.* (Nashville: Thomas Nelson Publishing, 2006), p.52.

47 Psalm 32:1-5

48 Genesis 3:15

49 II Samuel 11, 12

50 Proverbs 3:5

51 Manning, Brennan, *The Relentless Tenderness of Jesus* (Grand Rapids: Baker Book House, 2004), p. 48

52 Luke 1:28 (NKJV)

[53] Smedes, Lewis, *Shame and Grace* (New York: Harper Collins Publishing, 1993), pp. 107-108.

[54] Titus 2:11

[55] Matthew 11:28

[56] Colossians 2:13-14 (NASB)

[57] Psalm 103:12

[58] Jeremiah 31:34

[59] Ephesians 4:32

[60] May, Gerald, *Addiction and Grace* (New York: Harper Collins Publishing, 1988), p. 114.

[61] Taken from forgiveness handouts from Grace Ministries. Manassas, VA

[62] John 1:29

[63] John 8:31-32

[64] Philippians 4:8

[65] Ephesians 4:22-24; Romans 12:1-2

[66] Ephesians 6:13-14 (NASB)

[67] John 17:17

[68] Philippians 2:16

[69] I Peter 1:25

[70] Ephesians 2:1

[71] John 8:44

[72] Ephesians 6:10-11

[73] Backus, William, *Telling Yourself the Truth* (Minneapolis: Bethany House, 2000), p. 13

[74] II Corinthians 10:4-5

[75] Matthew 4:3

[76] Luke 22:42

[77] John 10:10; John 14:6

[78] Mark 8:34

[79] Foster, Richard. *Celebration of Discipline* (San Francisco: Harper Collins, 1998), p. 110.

[80] Mark 8:34

[81] Mark 1:17-18

[82] Philippians 3:4-11

[83] Proverbs 3:5

[84] Manning, Brennan. *Ruthless Trust* (San Francisco: Harper Collins, 2000), pp. 12-13.

[85] Job 2:9

[86] Job 2: 10

[87] Philippians 1:23

[88] Philippians 1:24-26

[89] Manning, Brennan. *Ruthless Trust* (San Francisco: Harper Collins, 2000). p. 5.

[90] Romans 7:24

[91] Comisky, Andy. *Living Waters: Pursuing Sexual and Relational Wholeness in Christ* (Anaheim, CA: Desert Stream Press, 2000), p. 48.

[92] Galatians 2:20

[93] Philippians 4:13

[94] Galatians 5:16, Romans 8:6,13

[95] Romans 8:37

[96] Schmemann, Alexander. *The Eucharist* (Crestwood, NY: St. Vladiimir's Seminary Press, 2003), p. 102.

[97] Payne, Leanne. *The Healing Presence* (Westchester, NY: Crossway, 1985), p. 95.

98 Curtis, Brent, Eldredge, John. *The Sacred Romance* (Nashville: Thomas Nelson Publishers, 1997), p. 73.

99 Genesis 2:18

100 Genesis 2:20

101 Genesis 2:20-22

102 Crabb, Larry. *The Marriage Builder* (Grand Rapids: Zondervan, 1992), p. 45.

103 Comiskey, Andy. *Living Waters: Pursuing Sexual and Relational Wholeness in Christ* (Anaheim, CA: Desert Stream Press, 2000), p. 109.

104 Comiskey, Andy. *Living Waters: Pursuing Sexual and Relational Wholeness in Christ* (Anaheim, CA: Desert Stream Press, 2000), p. 111.

105 Bonhoeffer, Dietrich. *Life Together* (San Francisco: Harper Collins, 1963), p. 23.

106 James 5:16

107 Proverbs 27:17

108 Ecclesiastes 4:9-12

109 I Peter 1:22

110 Hebrews 10:24-25

111 Jeremiah 17:9

112 Ezekiel 36:26

113 Temple, William. *Readings in St. John's Gospel, First Series* (London: Macmillan and Co., 1939), p. 68.

114 Weirsbe, Warren. *Real Worship* (Atlanta: Oliver Nelson and Co., 1986), p. 43.

115 I Samuel 12:24

116 Genesis 2:25

117 Foster, Richard. *Celebration of Discipline* (Harper Collins Publishers, San Francisco, 1998), p. 1.

118 Psalm 42:7

119 Mark 10:46-52

120 John 5:2-9

121 Psalm 37:4

122 Matthew 22:37-40

123 Swindoll, Charles. *So, You Want to Be Like Christ* (Nashville: Thomas Nelson, 2005), p. 9.

124 I Timothy 4:7

125 Hall, Mark. *Love Them Like Jesus* (Zoo Club Music, 2005).

126 Romans 8:28

127 II Corinthians 1:3-4

Breinigsville, PA USA
13 December 2010
251307BV00002B/1/P